The MIT Press

Cambridge, Massachusetts

London, England

International Constructivist Architecture, 1922–1939

Sima Ingberman

This book was set in Futura and Bodoni by DEKR
Corporation and was printed and bound in the
United States of America.

Library of Congress Cataloging-in-Publication Data

Ingberman, Sima.
    ABC : international constructivist architecture,
1922–1939 / Sima Ingberman.
        p.   cm.
    Includes bibliographical references and index.
    ISBN 0-262-09031-7
    1. Constructivism (Architecture)—History.
2. ABC Beiträge zum Bauen.   I. Title.
NA682.C65I54   1994
724′.6—dc20
                                93-36771
                                    CIP

For Nina, Avi, Efram, and Michael

Preface

Two ongoing misconceptions exist about the constructivist architecture of the 1920s, the first that constructivism was essentially a Russian phenomenon and the second that constructivism resulted in relatively few built buildings. ABC, the international constructivist movement, proves this assessment to be highly inaccurate.

These misconceptions evolved for good reason. Constructivism was the blanket term used to describe much of the new architecture (as well as the sculpture and art) that developed in postrevolutionary Russia between 1919 and 1930. Constructivism intended to symbolize the honest and vital spirit of the October Revolution by stressing an open approach to design that exposed the parts and materials of a building as dynamically as possible. One outstanding flaw characterized the unprecedented designs that constructivism inspired—they were often unbuilt if not unbuildable. As a result, constructivist architecture came to be seen mainly as an exuberant paper architecture that was usually expressive of Soviet ideology rather than the realities of building.

As Russia's architects were drawing their visions, an international constructivist faction, significantly different from any in the USSR, began to form outside of its borders in 1922. By 1924 it had organized under the name of ABC and soon resolved to bring constructivism into the lives of a multinational constituency. ABC's members intended their buildings to be built and adjusted the Soviet approach in order to make this possible. They were often successful. Between 1924 and 1939, the ABC architects designed highly original constructivist buildings for sites in Holland, Switzerland, Germany, Czechoslovakia, Russia, Mexico, and the United States. Many of these were built and some have since become landmarks of the modern movement.

The ABC movement began when El Lissitzky (b. 1890), the Soviet designer, recognized that constructivism deserved to be an international movement rather than a regional one. While in Berlin in 1922, he met the young Dutch architect Mart Stam (b. 1899) and shared this idea with him. Stam was instantly converted to constructivism, but not blindly. Stam recognized the impracticalities inherent in the Soviet designs and resolved to convert constructivism into an approach that was economically and structurally viable. Within months after meeting Lissitzky, Stam returned to Holland and enthusiastically shared his personal evaluation of constructivism with two visiting Swiss friends, the architects Hans Schmidt (b. 1893) and Werner Moser (b. 1896).

Schmidt and Moser returned to Switzerland that winter. Their experiences in Rotterdam inspired them to establish a nucleus of radical architecture in their homeland. Early in 1923, the two men invited the Swiss architects Hannes Meyer (b. 1889), Hans Wittwer (b. 1894),

Paul Artaria (b. 1892), and Emil Roth (b. 1893) to join their fledgling group. The following year the group was completed after a series of unrelated events brought Stam and Lissitzky to Switzerland. Impressed by the activities of Schmidt and his colleagues, the foreign visitors joined their alliance. Shortly thereafter, in the spring of 1924, they collectively established ABC, which went on to become the most significant architectural constructivist group outside the USSR.

Lissitzky returned to Russia in 1925. Two years later the Zurich architects Rudolf Steiger (b. 1900), Max Ernst Haefeli (b. 1901), and Karl Egender (b. 1897) affiliated themselves with the group. Although ABC's membership changed over the next decade, the ABC approach remained vital through 1939.

The ABC group deeded an extraordinary legacy that redefined and expanded the entire constructivist movement. This book chronicles ABC's accomplishments. It traces the events that led to ABC's formation and offers an overview of the movements's many buildings and projects. A broad survey, it underscores those features that place specific buildings within the parameters of ABC constructivism and cites their role within the movement.

This book differs from existing texts on ABC and its architects in one essential manner. With few exceptions that include Kenneth Frampton, scholars have recognized ABC only as the group that published the Swiss magazine *ABC Beiträge zum Bauen*, which was issued between 1924 and 1928. *ABC Beiträge zum Bauen* was acclaimed for its radical Neue Sachlichkeit approach to modernism and for its role in presenting new Russian designs to the West. The members of the group were viewed as little more than talented radical modernists who shared a common admiration of Russian constructivism and whose oeuvre sometimes reflected that admiration.

Stam, Meyer, Schmidt, Wittwer, and their ABC colleagues were not recognized as pioneers who had joined to develop an unprecedented constructivism in their own right. Consequently, *ABC Beiträge zum Bauen* was not understood as the guideline to their new international style but as just another avant-garde publication of that era. This oversight has robbed modernism of an essential chapter. It is the intention of this book to present an encompassing overview of the ABC contribution so that the ABC architects may finally receive the recognition their important efforts deserve.

Acknowledgments

There are several people to whom I am most indebted. I would like to thank Professor Kenneth Frampton of Columbia University for his extraordinary insights and ongoing encouragement, and Professor Eugene Santomasso of the Graduate Center of the City University of New York who first introduced me to ABC and went on to serve as my dissertation advisor. Without his excellent guidance and ongoing enthusiasm, my dissertation and subsequently this book could not have been written. I would also like to thank Professor Esther Crystal for friendship and assistance beyond any expected bounds.

The invaluable memories that Alfred Roth and the members of the (Emil) Roth, Schmidt, and Moser families shared with me have enriched my appreciation of ABC, and I am grateful for their generosity.

I would also like to thank Dr. Werner Oechslin, the director of the GTA at the Federal Institute of Technology in Zurich, for his invaluable cooperation, as well as the very capable Mrs. Therese Schweizer of the GTA. Roger Conover's confidence in my work certainly merits gratitude as well. Many thanks as well to Julia Bloomfield for wonderful advice, to Matthew Abbate, my very knowledgeable editor, and to Jeannet Leendertse, this book's designer. And I would like to acknowledge Walter Mair, the very gifted Swiss photographer who took all the contemporary photographs shown in this book.

I am also deeply indebted to my family and would like to thank my parents Sara and Bernard Blumenfeld, my sisters Miriam and Rachel and their families, my son-in-law Michael, and above all my children, Nina, Avi, and Efram, for their unfailing support throughout the years that this book was written.

One

El Lissitzky, Mart Stam, and the Birth of ABC Constructivism

1

El Lissitzky, the Father of International Constructivism

If any individual deserves to be called the father of international constructivism, it is El Lissitzky. Without his insistence that constructivism be an international rather than a Russian movement, it is quite possible that ABC would not have come into being. Any history of the ABC movement must therefore begin with Lissitzky and his unprecedented goals.

While it is commonly known that Lissitzky came to the West on behalf of the Soviet government, the true nature of his agenda is less often discussed. Lissitzky arrived in Berlin in the autumn of 1921 as an official emissary of the Soviet government. Most Europeans believed that the sole purpose of his mission was to promote the talents of his comrade artists—an obvious conclusion, since he did spend his days organizing art exhibitions, creating publications, and giving art-related lectures. Despite such evidence of goodwill, he had actually come to Europe on a far grander assignment. Lissitzky had been sent by his government to help prepare for a Communist takeover of Europe. Constructivist art and architecture were to be the means by which he was to introduce Europe's architects, artists, and intellectuals to the positive aspects of Communism.

By 1920, Vladimir Lenin had already decided to extend his sphere of influence outside the boundaries of the Soviet Union. He envisioned the spread of Communism throughout Europe. Although Lenin foresaw the "victory of the international Soviet republic," he also knew that his country was not prepared for a military invasion at that time. He thus conceived of a more practical plan that could be implemented immediately. Lenin and his party called for a preliminary cultural invasion that would produce strong admiration for the USSR among select Europeans. They expected this admiration to develop into a sense of allegiance that would prove most helpful when an actual military invasion did finally occur.

At the Second Congress of the Communist International (1920), Lenin's regime announced the formation of an international Proletkult that would develop the master plan for such a cultural assault. Anatole Lunacharsky, the Commissar of the Ministry of Education and the Arts, was chosen to oversee the Proletkult. Lunacharsky had a true understanding of the propaganda potential of postrevolutionary Russian art and architecture. He knew that the dramatic billboards, graphics, posters, stage productions, and constructions used to symbolize the spirit of the revolution had proven to be extremely powerful propaganda tools. They had certainly inspired zeal and support for the regime among Russia's largely illiterate populace.[1] The commissar believed that more sophisticated Soviet art forms, such as painting and sculpture, could create similar pro-Soviet sentiment among Europe's more urbane and educated constituency.

It was Lunacharsky's task to find the person who could launch this campaign in Europe. Remarkably enough he found him working at IZO, one of his own department's agencies. IZO, the Department of Figurative Arts, was established to strengthen ties with artists outside the country; a magazine, also named *IZO*, was published to promote this exchange. The magazine survived for only a single issue, but the impression its young editor, El Lissitzky, made on Lunacharsky lasted far longer.

The commissar realized that this young architect and designer differed from many of his provincial compatriots. Lissitzky had a truly international background and relished the idea of traveling and creating contacts within the larger global community. Born in 1890 in Polshinok, Russia, he had always sought broader horizons. He moved to Germany in 1909 to study architecture at Darmstadt's prestigious Polytechnic. During his student years he also traveled extensively throughout Europe and in 1911 visited Paris and many parts of Italy. The outbreak of the First World War prompted his return to Russia. He came home fluent in German and very well informed about avant-garde trends in Europe.

After his return, he developed new and experimental forms of artistic expression. Among these were the Prouns, highly original protoarchitectural graphic renderings that he was constantly refining (figures 1.1 and 1.2), as well as propaganda posters that allegorized the Revolution. The latter included "Beat the Whites with the Red Wedge" and "What Have You Done for the Front " of 1919. Lissitzky's interests lay not only in his own work. He joined collaborative organizations and accepted teaching positions that enabled him to interact with the growing ranks of Russia's constructivist architects and designers. So knowledgeable did he become that by 1921 he was regarded as a highly effective lecturer on the principles of the new Soviet art and architecture. Soon he was asked to teach the subject in Vitebsk, at the Art Cooperative, and later at the Vkhutemas (Higher Technical Art Studios), Moscow's most progressive technical academy. It was not long before he came to head the architecture faculty at the Vkhutemas. He also excelled at organizing exhibitions and participated in the ground-breaking Moscow show of the revolutionary new Soviet design, the Obmokhu. In addition to all of these traits, Lissitzky had a genuine talent for interacting with people and making new friends.

It was this combination of qualifications that convinced Lunacharsky to designate him Russia's cultural ambassador at large. Lissitzky, a devout Communist, was honored and saw his appointment as an exceptional challenge. Enthusiastically he prepared to return to Germany to undertake a mission no one had attempted previously.

El Lissitzky was, of course, not the first Russian to bring information on the cultural situation within the Soviet Union to the West. Konstantin Umansky, for example, a Vienna-based Soviet Tass correspondent, had made that introduction in 1919 when he published *Neue Kunst in Russland 1914–1919* (New Art in Russia 1914–1919). In January 1920, Umansky also delivered a speech in Vienna on Russian art and architecture and showed works by such up and coming Russians as Altman, Goncharova, Falk, Malevich, Rodchenko, and Tatlin. This lecture became a memorable event that was widely discussed in that city's artistic circles.

1.1
**"Proun 1A, Bridge 1," 1919,
by El Lissitzky.**

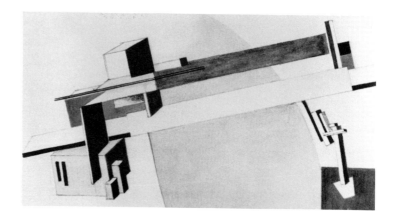

1.2
"Proun 1E, the Town," 1921,
by El Lissitzky.

By 1922, a noteworthy Russian expatriate colony had also developed in Berlin. This group included such eminent former members of the Soviet avant-garde as Chagall, Gabo, Pevsner, Altman, Ehrenburg, Kandinsky, and Meyerhold. They formed their own circle in the city and often met at the Romanisches Cafe or the House of Arts. Current trends in the Soviet arts were discussed there on a continual basis. Information on Russia's cultural and artistic trends was therefore available to anyone who was truly interested.

However, Europe's artistic community had not yet encountered any Russian of Lissitzky's magnitude. While other Russians had come to the West for a variety of reasons, no artist had yet arrived with such a master plan or such an approach. Lissitzky's ultimate goal was to unite architects and artists of many nationalities under the banner of Communism. Realizing that Communism was an intimidating word to many Europeans, he modified Communism to constructivism, a term understood as artistic rather than political. Accordingly he resolved to create an international constructivist network made up of influential members of the European avant-garde. Lissitzky knew that their opinions could ultimately induce the general population to see Soviet work and ideas in an affirmative light.

The first stop on Lissitzky's mission was Poland. He stayed in Warsaw for several days and made every effort to meet influential figures in the arts. He then allowed himself to be invited to deliver a lecture on Soviet art to an assembly that included that city's radical artists. As he had hoped, the lecture proved most effective and numerous artists were eager to make his acquaintance thereafter; Lissitzky formed several important friendships during his stay, including one with Henryk Berlewi, a leader of the Polish avant-garde.

After his success in Warsaw, Lissitzky was ready for Germany, a country that featured prominently in Lenin's master plan. He was to stay there for much of 1923, and it was there that his mission gathered force. Berlin was his first stop. Shortly after his arrival he contacted those Russian expatriates who had already settled in the city; they introduced him into Berlin's cultural circles. It did not take long for Lissitzky to find numerous new friends sympathetic to his work and ideas. Among these were Hans Richter and Viking Eggeling, two highly visible members of that city's avant-garde.

In order to expand his circle of admirers, he set about organizing a comprehensive exhibition that included paintings by Malevich, Rosanova, Kliun, and Popova, and three-dimensional constructions by Tatlin, Stenberg, Gabo, and Rodchenko. Lissitzky also included his protoarchitectural Prouns. This show, the "Erste russische Kunstausstellung" (First Exhibition of Russian Art), opened at the Van Diemen Gallery in Berlin in October 1922. In conjunction with the exhibition, Lissitzky lectured on the "New Russian Art"; both were extremely well received by the audience he was looking to attract.

The following spring he traveled with the exhibition to Amsterdam. Again he gave his inspiring lecture and this time drew the admiration of the De Stijl group. Theo van Doesburg became a lasting friend thereafter. Later that year the show traveled to Hannover, Germany, and was shown at the Kestner Society. Among the admirers Lissitzky gathered there was Sophie Küppers, his future wife.

By 1923 Lissitzky's name was known throughout European artistic circles, and not only for his exhibitions and lectures. Many of the most progressive artists had become familiar with his ideas through the International Faction of Constructivists and the magazine *Veshch, Gegenstand, Objet*. Within months of arriving in Germany, he had made strenuous efforts to form a group that was publicly willing to support his cause. The group thus formed agreed to call itself the International Faction of Constructivists; Lissitzky soon put their new loyalty to advantageous use.

In May 1922, the First International Congress of Progressive Artists was held in Düsseldorf. It attracted hundreds of artists of assorted nationalities and points of view. Berlin's November Group, members of the Darmstadt Secession, and the Young Rhineland Group from

Düsseldorf were all represented. Making its official debut here was the International Faction of Constructivists. This group surprised the entire Congress. Suddenly artists such as van Doesburg, Richter, Eggeling, and Baumann were supporting a cause that hardly anyone had heard of before. Lissitzky's new brigade was highly vocal. Announcing that they represented constructivist groups from Romania, Switzerland, Scandinavia, and Germany, they issued a manifesto and proclamations. These stressed "comradely" collectivity and the role of art in reorganizing society. Additionally, the Dutch De Stijl group issued a separate statement in which its members aligned themselves with the new constructivist brigade.

Lissitzky saw the International Faction of Constructivists as a bridge to a larger audience throughout Europe and the Americas—an audience that could best be reached via publications. At the Congress he laid the foundation for an international network of small constructivist magazines that would be printed throughout the West after the Congress adjourned. These were to be modeled after the new magazine he had just issued in Berlin, *Veshch, Gegenstand, Objet* (figure 1.3), and would spread his gospel.

To let his latest venture become widely known, he introduced himself at the Congress as the editor of *Veshch, Gegenstand, Objet*. In a speech to the assembled artists, he outlined *Veshch*'s intention to unite the leaders of the new art on an international scale and to inform them of the extraordinary cultural and political developments in the USSR.[2] Copies of the publication, which was only a month old, were available at the conference. *Veshch* was awe-inspiring by any standards; nothing like it had been seen by this or any other audience. It featured a striking and unprecedented integration of typography, graphics, and examples of Soviet art that varied from page to page. Equally impressive was its message. The publication was trilingual (Russian, German, and French) and contained gripping editorials that called for the unification of all artists under the latest avant-garde phenomenon, constructivism, and for support of the country whose ideology was best suited to modern life, the USSR.

1.3

**First page of *Veshch,
Gegenstand, Objet*, no. 3
(1922).**

Veshch was Lissitzky's highly stylized plea for a global Communist community.

Ever the enterprising visionary, Lissitzky hoped that his new followers would create a host of *Veshch* imitations worldwide. They did not disappoint him. Many members of Lissitzky's new circle responded affirmatively at the Congress or shortly thereafter. The editors of *De Stijl* immediately offered to publish the statements of the International Faction of Constructivists as a gesture of allegiance to Lissitzky. Another preexisting publication, the Hungarian art journal *MA*, followed suit thereafter. Their actions set a trend in motion. Within two years, an entire pro-constructivist network of small magazines that included *Zenit* (Belgrade), *Stavba* (Prague), *Disk* (Prague), and the Polish magazines *Block* and *Praesens* was established. These periodicals published gestures of support to Lissitzky in the form of articles or graphics by the Russian himself, or other examples of the new Soviet art.

Several literary and artistic personalities who edited their own magazines took a personal interest in Lissitzky as well. Harold Loeb and Matthew Josephson, the editors of *Broom,* the American journal that was created to forge cultural bridges between the United States and Europe, asked Lissitzky to design *Broom's* June 1923 cover. It proved so popular that he was asked to do three more that year. Kurt Schwitters, the German artist and editor of *Merz,* was equally impressed with the Russian and asked him to contribute to *Merz's* July 1923 and April-July 1924 editions. For the latter, Lissitzky designed the cover, the front and back pages, and even wrote an article entitled "Nasci" (Nature).

The combined effect of all this publicity created an international fascination with constructivism. But despite the positive attention, one feature was not well covered; all the magazines focused on Russia's art and not on its equally noteworthy architectural contribution. Neither *Veshch* nor *G,* the German magazine Lissitzky and Hans Richter launched in 1923, focused on constructivist architecture. This is not to say that G did not discuss avant-garde architecture. It did, for example, reproduce early work of Mies van der Rohe, but it did not really focus on radical Soviet buildings. In both content and form, G was usually reminiscent of the ecumenical *Veshch*. There, as in the other publications of the constructivist network, architecture had become a much neglected stepchild. It was up to Lissitzky to rectify the situation.

2

Lissitzky and Asnova

El Lissitzky was obligated to publicize constructivist architecture for two reasons. First, because any comprehensive overview of the USSR's cultural contribution had to include architecture. And secondly, he owed it to his fellow Asnova architects to promote their work.

Russia's constructivist architects did not necessarily agree on their interpretation of constructivism, and as a result several factions within this larger movement developed. Asnova, the New Association of Architects, evolved into the most abstract and theoretically inclined constructivist group in Russia. Organized in Moscow in 1923 under the leadership of Nikolai Ladovsky, Nikolai Dokuchayev, and Vladimir Krinsky, its oeuvre became synonymous with a lack of

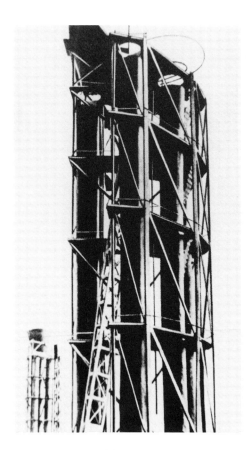

1.4

"Study in the Representation of Solid and Void, Tower for the Manufacture of Alkaline Solutions," 1922, by J. Gruschenko.

regard for the pragmatic realities of building. Instead Asnova emphasized the symbolic, emotive, and perceptual potential it saw in architecture.

While still at the Vkhutemas in Moscow in 1922, Lissitzky befriended Ladovsky and many of the other future Asnova members. Although the group did not officially organize until after his departure, he was already involved in the planning stages that precipitated its formation. He saw his own early work as representative of Asnova ideology and believed that his Prouns were reflective of this position.

Lissitzky implied as much in a lecture he delivered on September 21, 1921, at the Inkhuk, the Institute of Artistic Culture in Moscow. There he emphasized that Prouns were symbolic entities that used suprematist forms and their inherent properties to convey distinct messages. Each shape, color, and material was symbolic of an emotion or a state of being. Circles, for example, were equivalents of the earthly globe and connoted infinity. Black and white represented the "supportive character of the human condition," while the latter's "subjective character" was expressed in green, orange, violet, etc.

Lissitzky also stressed the relationship between architecture and theories of perception. Stating that he had studied Albert Einstein's theory of particular and general relativity, he intended to demonstrate the application of relativity theory to architecture. Einstein had proved that there was a fourth dimension, time. Lissitzky accordingly resolved to design "not in three dimensions, but in four." Prouns and other constructions were therefore rendered in a multidimensional floating state not locked into any single time frame. As a result, a viewer could "walk around [a construction], look at it from above, study it from beneath."[3]

Lissitzky's work did have much in common with the ideals of other future Asnova members and with the work of Ladovsky and his Vkhutemas students. At the Moscow academy, Ladovsky had instructed his students to design utilitarian structures with the elements of composition exposed. The fulfillment of pragmatic requirements was not considered of primary importance. What was essential was the manner in which elementarist forms and structural parts were combined for perceptual and symbolic effects. In addition, students were encouraged to exhibit multiple views of each project. Along these prescribed lines, Ladovsky's students designed factories, piers, and other utilitarian concerns. Because these student projects were valued as "space volume studies," their functional properties often received only secondary recognition in their titles.

A typical example of such student work was a highly stylized production center for lye by J. Gruschenko (1922; figure 1.4). Gruschenko showed minimal interest in the realistic aspects of his project. His primary concern was in the artistic arrangement of elementarist volumes, such as the drum, and in a presentation that permitted several viewpoints. The title, "Study in the Representation of Solid and Void, Tower for the Manufacture of Alkaline Solutions," reflected the architect's priorities.

1.5
"Restaurant on a Cliff over a Lake: Exercise in the Representation of Formal Qualities of Mass and Equilibrium," 1922, by W. Simbirchev.

Another Ladovsky student project was Simbirchev's suspended restaurant (1922), which was entitled "Restaurant on a Cliff over a Lake: Exercise in the Representation of Formal Qualities of Mass and Equilibrium" (figure 1.5). Essentially the work stressed the spatial organization of suprematist shapes within an exposed frame and the diagonal elevation of the restaurant in order to allow for multiple perspectives. The dynamic thrust of abstract forms, not the feasibility of its construction, was the architect's concern here.

Lissitzky was already in Europe when Ladovsky, Dokuchayev, and Krinsky were joined by A. Efimov, I. Mochalov, and several others to officially form Asnova. At best, he was limited to a corresponding membership. To atone for his lack of active participation, Lissitzky resolved to bring Asnova to the attention of the West. (It was not until his return to the USSR that he assumed an active role. In 1926, with Ladovsky's assistance, he edited the sole issue of the group's publication, *Izvestia Asnova*.) By the early months of 1924, Lissitzky was most eager to launch a European architectural publication that would focus on Russian constructivism, especially on the works of Asnova.

Early in 1924, the opportunity he had been looking for finally presented itself. It came in the form of Mart Stam, the young Dutch architect with Communist convictions and radical architectural ideas whom Lissitzky had first met in Berlin in 1922. Profoundly influenced by Lissitzky, Stam returned to his native Rotterdam an advocate of constructivism. They corresponded; not long after, illness brought them together again. In 1923, the Russian contracted a life-threatening case of pulmonary tuberculosis. His doctors insisted that he retire to a sanitarium for an extensive cure, and in early 1924 he departed for Locarno, a resort in southern Switzerland, stopping in Zurich en route.

Stam was then working in that city; along with a group of Swiss colleagues, he was eager to start an architectural magazine. The group included Hans Schmidt, Paul Artaria, Hannes Meyer, and Hans Wittwer of Basel, Emil Roth, an Italian-born Swiss national, and Werner Moser, originally of Zurich but working for Frank Lloyd Wright in the United States at the time. Their new publication planned to focus solely on radical contemporary trends in architecture. Unfortunately, neither Stam nor any of his friends had any knowledge of magazine publication and needed guidance.

Stam greeted Lissitzky at Zurich's train station and soon explained his group's predicament. Recognizing his hoped-for opportunity, Lissitzky offered his support immediately. Throughout his stay in Zurich, the two discussed the new project, and Stam introduced Lissitzky to some of his future Swiss collaborators. After Lissitzky's departure, Stam and his colleagues visited him in Locarno. During these visits their new publication, *ABC Beiträge zum Bauen*, was planned.

Lissitzky believed that he had finally found the podium he was seeking for Asnova in *ABC*. Although the Europeans were only planning a radical platform instead of an openly constructivist one, Lissitzky knew that Stam's friends were supportive of Communism and constructivism. It was therefore Lissitzky's intention first to convince Stam to declare himself a constructivist, rather than just a modernist whose work was strongly influenced by Russian ideas, and then to enlist his help in persuading the others to do the same.

The Russian's plan succeeded. With Stam's help, Lissitzky's new European friends became converts; Lissitzky wasted little time in educating them to the merits of Asnova constructivism in particular. To insure continued interest and future loyalty, Lissitzky also invited Stam and Emil Roth, one of the Swiss who frequently accompanied Stam on his Locarno visits, to become foreign members of Asnova. Both felt honored and accepted readily.

An agreement was soon reached between Lissitzky, Stam, and the architects Stam represented. Lissitzky offered to guide the Swiss group in starting a new magazine. In return he expected *ABC* to print an editorial openly supporting Asnova and to show mainly Asnova works when discussing the new Soviet architecture. Lissitzky promised his new partners unpublished examples of his own work as well as numerous Asnova projects that had never been seen in the West. The Russian also encouraged the group to join the network of small international constructivist magazines that he promoted. Stam and the Swiss group accepted his offer and an alliance was formed.

3

Mart Stam's Vision

The ABC-Asnova alliance should have been a most contradictory one. Mart Stam was, by all accounts, a radical functionalist whose ideas were at odds with some of Asnova's fundamental principles. Stam prided himself on an approach that was deliberately free of symbolic, decorative, or overtly stylized elements that had no functional justification. Architecture for him was the sum of functions and materials presented in as simple and economical a manner as possible. In fact he openly made this point in one of his seminal essays:

*Each new task gives us the chance to abandon aesthetic consid-
erations, to forget beauty of external proportion and to study the
project from a purely functional point of view. . . . Best things
are always those remarkable only for their unpretentious righ-
teousness. The important element in any undertaking is not that
which betrays its creator, the designer, but only what is functional and impersonal.*[4]

In the name of architectural honesty Stam sought to develop a means
of architectural expression that relied on an exposed structural system, a blatant revelation of the interior's workings, and the outward
expression of a floor plan that was based solely on functional considerations. A strong proponent of mass production, he advocated
modular repetition of constructional elements within building plans.
In addition, he intended that his buildings reveal the materials of
which they were constructed.

Stam hardly invented many of these concepts; they were already
integral to Dutch modernism by the time he finished his schooling.
Born on August 5, 1899, in Purmerend, the Netherlands, and educated at the State School for Draftsmanship between 1917 and 1919,
he came to look to such masters of Dutch modernism as Berlage,
Oud, Bijvoet, and Duiker for inspiration. In 1922 he wrote a series
of essays, published the following year in the *Schweizerische Bauzeitung,* that explained his admiration of these men. Excerpts from
some of these reveal the sources for Stam's own approach and prove
how rooted he was in the functional tradition that had evolved in
Holland since the turn of the century.

The first essay stressed the fundamentals of H. P. Berlage's legacy
to modernism. Berlage, Stam claimed, had liberated architecture
from the superficialities of the beaux-arts and had promoted "an
architecture of rational and truthful revelation" where each space
had "a designated function" and "received its own interior and
exterior articulation." Berlage's buildings, Stam wrote, "clearly expressed the materials of construction and the constructional system."

Also of interest to him was Berlage's advocacy of technological imagery and standardization.[5]

Stam's other essays documented contemporary ideals that derived from the precedents Berlage had established. For example, Berlage's Borse had instituted the use of a technological vocabulary, particularly on the interiors, that relied on openly exposed structural and technological parts. Such details later inspired Stam to write:

Technology has endowed . . . buildings with the ability to bespeak their [technical] functions. As examples one usually thinks of silos, bridges, and factories. And one thinks of such creations of technology as autos, machines, locomotives, and battleships. . . . Now, however, we must grasp the fact that technological articulation is not limited to these. We must learn to express our buildings in similar terms.[6]

Among the younger generation of architects worthy of distinction, Stam cited J. J. P. Oud and the partnership of Bijvoet and Duiker. Oud was cited for his development of standardized modular plans for garden developments and row houses in Rotterdam. Meeresstrand (1922) was chosen as an example of the latter. Bijvoet and Duiker were recognized for their functional ground plans and the cubic exteriors that expressed those plans.[7]

From these articles it becomes increasingly clear that Stam already advocated a doctrinaire functionalism by 1922. Given Stam's dedication to so radical a position, it comes as a shock that he would align himself with Lissitzky and Asnova in a magazine that was to represent his own point of view. Surprisingly, however, Stam saw no contradiction in such a union. In fact, by 1924 he believed that Asnova's and Russian constructivism's explicit manner of expressing the parts, materials, and functions of a building was most suitable for the approach he had been formulating since his meetings with Lissitzky in Berlin in 1922.

Stam had moved temporarily to Berlin in 1922 and worked successively in the offices of Hans Poelzig and Max Taut. He soon developed a fascination with the avant-garde society of that city and spent his nonworking hours acquainting himself with artists and designers. An ardent Communist, Stam was particularly intrigued by the expatriate Russians in Berlin. To broaden his knowledge of Russian architecture he sought out the man the avant-garde of the city was currently discussing, the newly arrived El Lissitzky. It did not take long for Lissitzky to introduce him to Russian constructivism and the work of Tatlin, Ladovsky, and Ladovsky's students. By the time Stam left Berlin in the fall of 1922, he had become a staunch proponent of constructivism, but not exactly of Lissitzky's kind.

In Berlin Stam had developed a distinctly personal appreciation of Russian constructivism. His evaluation of its merits was seen largely through a functional point of view. Totally disinterested in the theoretical aspects of Asnova's gospel, he saw constructivism as a means of further emphasizing those aspects of construction he considered most vital: the materials, components, and methods of construction. Stam was also impressed by the manner in which the Soviet buildings flaunted technological innovations and communications paraphernalia.

Stam's selective appreciation of Russian constructivism was explained in an essay he wrote at a later date. There he recalled his distinct impression of the material Lissitzky had shown him during their meetings in Berlin. Of constructivism and the projects of the Vkhutemas architects (atelier Ladovsky) and Tatlin he wrote:

In the sculpture of that time enclosed volume gives way to space—created by wire, rods, straight and curved surfaces. Transparent volume evolves. They know that the sun turns in space, that shadows continually alter, that men move. . . . The architects trained by the Vkhutemas developed projects: repre-

sentations of space, hanging from a cliff linked by steps and ca-
ble cars. Tatlin entered a competition with revolving mobile
lecture rooms.[8]

Stam lauded these works only for their open, lightweight, and sometimes transparent volumes, their use of such tensile equipment as
antennae, their marked emphasis on all circulatory parts, and their
incorporation of such mobile innovations as cable cars. He did not
mention any of the theoretical principles that Asnova used to justify
such constructions. Stam thus did not see a conflict in accepting
Asnova; for him it was a bold means of exposing the functions and
components of a building more honestly than any other approach
had done to date. Stam believed that constructivism, if properly
edited, could enable him to create absolute functional structures.

TWO

The Swiss Agenda

1

Schmidt and Moser in Rotterdam

The above information explains why Stam was able to accept Lissitzky's ideas so readily, but it does not answer another question. If Stam had found a Russian approach that lent itself well to Dutch adaptation, why did he ally himself with a Swiss group and seek to promote his ideas in a Swiss magazine? The answer lies in the curious circumstances that produced the strong bond between Stam and two young Swiss architects he encountered in Rotterdam in 1922.

When they met Stam there in the early part of that year, Hans Schmidt and Werner Moser were in Rotterdam on the advice of the renowned Swiss professor Karl Moser. More than any other Swiss pedagogue of his time, Karl Moser was responsible for attempting to train young Swiss architects in the vernacular of modernism. But by 1922 Karl

Moser admitted that it was sometimes necessary to leave Switzerland in order to achieve that goal.

The father of Werner, Karl Moser was both a highly successful architect and a revered faculty member of Switzerland's premier architecture academy, the Federal Institute of Technology (ETH) in Zurich. Unlike many of his contemporaries, he was anxious to move beyond the rigid confines of classicism and historicism that characterized Swiss architecture during and after the turn of the century. Accordingly, he developed a reductive, planar, and nonornamental version of the beaux-arts style that stressed abstraction and clarity. The Badischer Station in Basel (1912) is a fine example of this approach.

Over the next ten years Moser came to realize that his oeuvre was not revolutionary enough to inspire the development of any large-scale modern movement in Switzerland. By 1920 it was clear to him that modernism was based on a clear articulation of materials and structure, a lack of traditional ornament, and the clear external expression of a ground plan that was based solely on functional considerations. He saw these values realized in the work of others far better than in his own. Eager that his students follow the correct path toward modernism, he advised them to emulate foreign mentors whose ideas had already spawned successful modern movements.[1]

In a brave gesture, Moser wrote an article for the Swiss magazine *Das Werk* in which he openly stated his admiration for those whom he saw as the trailblazers of modernism, the Dutch architects H. P. Berlage and W. M. Dudok. He lauded Berlage for "design schemes based only on what was practical and suitable for each situation," noting "construction methods, layout, and materials" as well as the relationship of Berlage's buildings to the surrounding environment. He complimented Dudok, the man he saw as Berlage's disciple, for ground plans that were based solely on practical and logical needs and for the manner in which assorted functions were granted external differentiation.[2]

As Moser was the most progressive member of the ETH faculty, he attracted a following among the most radical members of the student body. They formed a loyal circle that valued his teachings as well as his personal advice. Prior to 1920, this circle included Moser's son Werner, Hans Schmidt, Emil Roth, and Hans Wittwer; later were added the younger architects Max Ernst Haefeli, Karl Egender, and Rudolf Steiger. All of these would form the core of ABC.

Disillusioned by the failure of a strong modernist tradition to develop in his native land, Moser openly told members of his circle that there was currently no place for them or for himself in Switzerland. In 1920, he announced that he was temporarily leaving Switzerland for the land of his modernist models and convinced his son and Hans Schmidt to follow him to Holland. Their departure was hardly surprising; other aspiring avant-garde Swiss architects had resorted to such a move far earlier. Edouard Jeanneret, the future Le Corbusier, dissatisfied with prevailing reactionary attitudes, had migrated to France during the First World War. Hannes Meyer, who had studied at the Basel Technical School, left for Berlin in 1908 to complete his education at the Kunstgewerbeschule. And Hans Wittwer, after graduating from the ETH in 1916, departed for England to study working-class housing prototypes there. The two Mosers and Hans Schmidt now joined the ranks of these expatriates.

The three men settled in Rotterdam and wasted little time in integrating themselves into life there. Karl Moser, on sabbatical, pursued his private agenda, while both young men found positions in architectural firms. Hans Schmidt joined the office of Brinkman, and Werner Moser found a position with Granpre Moliere, Verhangen and Kok. At work, Werner Moser met and befriended a fellow young employee, Mart Stam. Moser introduced Stam to Schmidt, who was equally taken with the young Dutchman. Stam soon became their closest friend in Rotterdam and rapidly evolved into their mentor.

Mart Stam was an outspoken and acknowledged Communist. In Holland, this did not alienate him from the larger artistic community since other prominent architects and artists shared his beliefs. Jan Wills, Robert van't Hoff, Gerrit Rietveld, Peter Alma, Theo van Doesburg, and Chris Beekman were all active Communists at the time. Stam went on to introduce his Swiss friends to young Communists in the arts.

Schmidt, in particular, was truly inspired by the new political climate. In Basel, he, his brother Georg, and friends such as Hannes Meyer formed a small pro-Communist core that was not tolerated by the reigning cultural elite. Switzerland was not hospitable to any Communist activity and only Basel had an active Communist organization, one comprised largely of workers. Swiss artists and architects were usually tradition-oriented in both their work and their political beliefs. At home Schmidt had always felt out of his element. Now, surrounded by like-minded Dutch company, his political convictions gained momentum.

A strengthened predisposition to Communism was certainly not the only benefit of the Swiss friends' Dutch sojourn. As Karl Moser's students, they shared his understanding of the necessary principles of modernism. From his writings, it is clear that Stam agreed with many of these. Stam went on to introduce Schmidt and Moser to additional radical Dutch architectural works that further emphasized rational planning, structure, and materials in a reductive and economical manner.

Several months after the arrival of the visitors, Stam departed for Berlin and did not come back until autumn. Upon his return, he informed Schmidt and Moser of his meetings with Lissitzky and his personal evaluation of the constructivist designs that the Russian had shown him. He also brought back two projects he had drafted in Berlin that were already indicative of his interpretation of constructivism. Mart Stam did not develop actual ABC constructivist prototypes until 1924, but these works emphasized two points that would characterize his later style: externalized structure and highly visible circulatory sections.

Stam went to great lengths to reveal internal structure on the exterior of Königsberg, one of his Berlin projects (figure 2.1). For Königsberg, a reinforced concrete building, Stam proposed an interior portal frame structural system, which he preferred for its flexibility, strength, economy, and its clear expression of the constructional process. The portal frame made it possible to see exactly how the slab rested on its support. Eager to express this support system externally as well, Stam deliberately created a facade that exaggerated floor slabs far more than necessary. Königsberg did not have load-bearing walls and could have accommodated a curtain wall, but Stam consciously did not use one. Instead, he foreshortened the vertical span of the windows to allow for broad bands of concrete between the floors. These were intended to allude to the floor slabs within. In reality, the bands did not correspond to the dimensions of the slabs, as they were much thicker. This gesture represented Stam's effort to grant external identity to such particulars of structure as floor slabs.

In addition to a revealing structure, Russian constructivist buildings tended to segregate specific functions within the overall building complex. Functions were given their own sections, as in the case of the circulatory shafts in which stairwells and elevators were housed. To further emphasize the importance of circulation, the Russians resorted to bridges or other technologically advanced means of transport to link building sections. In his Berlin projects Stam followed their example. Königsberg was consistently spliced by protruding circulatory sections. At Am Knie, another Berlin design of 1922, in addition to using similar towers Stam added a vivid network of glass-enclosed bridges to link the larger complex. The Am Knie complex employed the repetitive perimeter block format that was popular in Holland at this time (figure 2.2).

In December 1922, Schmidt's and Moser 's Dutch idyll came to an end. Schmidt went home to his native Basel and Werner Moser returned to Zurich, where his father awaited him. They brought with them a newly reinforced respect for functionalism and Communism, and above all a growing understanding of radical modernism that was markedly influenced by Stam's developing ideas.

KONSTRUKTIONSSCHEMA GESCHÄFTSHAUS – KÖNIGSBERG M. STAM

7

2.2

Am Knie project, 1922, by Mart Stam. From *ABC Beiträge zum Bauen*, series 2, no. 3 (1926), p. 3.

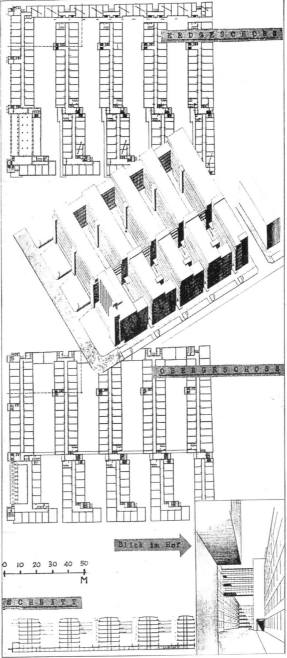

BERLIN.

Wettbewerbsentwurf für ein Bureauhaus am Knie.

Die Wettbewerbsaufgabe forderte eine grösste Anzahl von Bureauräumen mit der Möglichkeit beliebiger Unterteilung, Vermietung und Zugänglichkeit in einzelnen Gruppen. Der Entwurf verwirft die übliche geschlossene Anlage mit Innenhöfen und setzt dafür ein System offen aufgestellter Trakte mit offenen, von der Strasse direkt zu betretenden Höfen und weitgehenden Zugangsmöglichkeiten im Anschluss an die gegebene Situation.

2

Momentum Builds in Switzerland, 1922–1924

Hans Schmidt arrived in Basel precisely at the time that a competition was being held for the buildings of the Hornli Cemetery in that city. Fueled by optimism, he drafted and submitted an entry. Hannes Meyer, his friend, entered as well (figure 2.3). Schmidt's entry was eliminated during the first round and Meyer's fared little better. Their rejection was not based entirely on a disapproval of their talents. It was a political gesture as well.

Schmidt, his brother Georg, and Meyer had not hidden their ideological stance from Basel's cultural establishment. Meyer, in fact, was a well-known socialist who was making his presence known throughout Europe. In 1914 he had joined the socialist Swiss Co-Operative (Co-Op) Union. The Co-op Union promoted a communal

way of life based on the collective ownership of housing and land and the division of labor among residents. All educational, recreational, and health-related concerns were the responsibility of the commune. The Co-op Union also subsidized a variety of art-related activities and supported numerous artists, among them Meyer. Between 1923 and 1926 he designed display windows, product packaging, linoleum cuts, and theater sets for the movement.

Meyer's responsibilities within the movement soon extended beyond local concerns. By 1923, the Swiss Co-Op had designated him its official international arts envoy. The position required him to record the art-related activities of other international co-op networks. Meyer traveled throughout Europe; his observations resulted in over thirteen essays on the subject that were later printed in such publications as *Das Werk* and *MA*. Later, *ABC Beiträge zum Bauen* devoted the entire first issue of its second series (1926) to Meyer's analysis of European art and sculpture. (Most of the artists chosen for this issue had constructivist ties either stylistically or ideologically.)

So infuriated was Schmidt by his rejection and Meyer's that he called for retaliatory action. He believed it was time to fight the establishment in order to create an acknowledged place for radical modernists, particularly leftist ones, within Switzerland's architectural community. Since this was a task he could not undertake alone, Schmidt gathered a circle of like-minded men to assist him in this effort.

Early in 1923, Schmidt called a meeting to discuss his plan. In addition to his brother and Meyer, he invited fellow Basel radicals Hans Wittwer and Paul Artaria, his future partner. Shortly after returning to Basel, he had unexpectedly met Emil Roth, a former ETH friend, in an architectural office and asked him to come as well. Hoping for more than just a representation of local architects, he contacted Werner Moser in Zurich and asked him to bring several sympathetic colleagues from his area. Moser arrived with Max Ernst Haefeli and Rudolf Steiger, younger friends who were also students of his father's at the ETH. The meeting took place one weekend in a house Artaria had designed south of the Bielersee, a lake in the Swiss countryside.[3]

The existing situation in Switzerland was deplored at this meeting. The discussion focused on the Swiss government's interest in upperclass needs and how the architectural establishment pandered to these interests by producing edifices that monumentalized elitist power and taste. As a result, such neoclassical and traditional vernacular types as the Pfister Brothers' 1922 Winterthur Canton School and Otto Ingold's 1915 Volkshaus in Bern had come to dominate the architecture of the period. Too little emphasis had been placed on modern architecture and better mass housing, despite rioting by frustrated workers in Basel. Nor had adequate attention been given to planning proposals related to the needs of industry, traffic, and recreational facilities for the lower classes, which the group saw as core issues of contemporary city living.

The fledgling group called for the formation of a Swiss architectural network that would develop a modernist architecture capable of addressing social concerns where necessary. What style of modern architecture were they speaking of? Designs of this period by Schmidt and Roth reveal specific protoconstructivist details, and it is therefore entirely possible that they were already inspired by Stam's Berlin projects.

Between 1922 and 1924, the work of Schmidt and his friends underwent a highly visible metamorphosis. Since Karl Moser had trained most of them, their early work was rooted in abstract classicism, as Meyer's Hornli entry and Emil Roth's 1918 classically inspired plans for his Hotel am Schanzengraben proved. The senior Moser's examples did not call for the external articulation of individual functions, and accordingly these projects followed suit. But after Rotterdam, not only did various members' works become increasingly flat-roofed, simplified, and planar, but they also began to emphasize distinct constructivist features. A drawing by Hans Schmidt from 1922 shows that he had developed a strong interest in defining circulatory towers and shafts at this time (figure 2.4). The International Workers' Bureau project for Geneva of 1923, later shown in the *ABC* magazine, underscores this predisposition as well. (Its linked perimeter block formations also recall Stam's Am Knie plan.)[4] Similar tendencies also appear in the work of Emil Roth, such as his project for the Canton School in Winterthur (1922–1923; figure 2.5). The Canton School stair tower is given a distinct profile, while the overall composition is divided into several blocks according to functions, rather than standing as a single entity. Roth's earlier work lacked both of these qualities. Since Roth had not worked or studied in Holland, it is possible that Schmidt had inspired these changes.

To gather support for their aspiring network and their evolving new style, the architects resolved to undertake a propaganda campaign that would bring their cause before the public. An appropriate means for this endeavor was soon found, with the help of Mart Stam.

Still impressed with their Rotterdam friend, the Moser family invited Stam to work in the senior Moser's architectural firm in Zurich in 1923; he eagerly accepted their offer. The Mosers made a similar proposal to Emil Roth, who also accepted. Once in Zurich, Stam resumed his friendship with Werner Moser, befriended Roth, and reunited with Schmidt. The three Swiss architects shared their aspirations with Stam; with his assistance they proceeded to formulate

2.4
Untitled drawing, 1922, by
Hans Schmidt, from the Hans
Schmidt Archive, Federal
Institute of Technology, Zurich.

2.5
Canton School in Winterthur
project, 1922, by Emil Roth.

a plan of action. It was determined that the group's interests were best served by a publicity campaign within a widely read architectural magazine. The purpose of this campaign was to be twofold. First, readers had to be educated as to the merits of functional design via a series of general articles. After such a preparatory stage, they would be introduced to the group's work.

Fortunately, Stam and Schmidt were able to implement this plan. Since 1922, Stam had been writing essays on contemporary Dutch architecture that discussed the functional antecedents of modernism, often in relation to socialist ideals. Schmidt translated these into German and submitted them to the Swiss engineering and architectural journal *Schweizerische Bauzeitung;* through October and November of 1923 four articles entitled "Holland und die Baukunst unserer Zeit" (Holland and the Architecture of Our Time) were published.

The first piece discussed Berlage and his functional program. The second, subtitled "Der Haag'sche Kreis" (The Hague Circle), featured the previously cited projects of Bijvoet and Duiker, Oud, Dudok, and Stam. Oud and Dudok were known socialists and Stam a Communist. One week later, "Der Amsterdam'sche Kreis" (The Amsterdam Circle) presented an analysis of exemplary workers' housing projects by Kramer, Staal, and de Klerk that had been commissioned by the municipality of Amsterdam. Stam's final installment was devoted to town planning, "Stadtbau." Here he discussed his plan for a Hague extension and a plan by his former employer, Granpre Moliere, Verhangen and Kok, for a Rotterdam sector. Both plans described the upgrading of commercial, recreational, and working-class residential sectors in these cities.[5]

Jubilant that an established periodical was publicizing the issues and works that they supported, the group hoped for additional recognition in future issues. But within weeks of Stam's fourth article their crusade came to an abrupt halt. In December the *Schweizerische Bauzeitung* suddenly denounced Stam and his cause. In a review of Stam's published essays, E. Wipf stated:

This Dutch architect believes that the architecture of our land could develop along the lines of the architecture of his land. . . . This cannot be the case; our traditions, our terrain, our climate, and our indigenous building materials are not the same as those of our neighbors. . . . It is important to fight such foreign influences; they can only mislead us. If we heed them they will lead us to create buildings that do not suit our areas and our land. . . . We must not abandon our own needs, our own traditions.[6]

Wipf's critique was merely a prelude to what was to follow in later issues. On January 5, 1924, Armin Meili, a prominent Lucerne architect, published an article "Wir und die Architektur des Auslands" (Foreign Architecture and Us) in which Mart Stam and his ideas were once again deplored. Meili proclaimed:

Why should not we Swiss determine the nature of the future Swiss works? . . . The source of today's temptation is the Dutch school. . . . Although their windmills are wonderful . . . Mart Stam's digressions show the final results of a serious development. One which is rarely spiritual in the building solutions it seeks. . . . Regardless of whether or not the Dutch pursuit of the rational or the fantastic has validity, let them not bring their quest to our soil.[7]

Meili's attack did not end here. The following week another article championed Swiss traditionalism and praised such acceptable foreign influences as Oestberg's Town Hall in Stockholm.[8]

These denunciations signaled the group's fall from grace. It had lost its podium and consequently its potential for future recognition. Humiliated and angry, the group refused to terminate its crusade and resolved to take a new course of action. In February 1924, the members discussed the possibility of publishing a magazine of their own and sought experienced guidance.

3

The Formation of a Group and the Birth of a Magazine

Early in 1924, Mart Stam asked El Lissitzky to join their venture. For purposes of recognition and solidarity, Meyer, Wittwer, Roth, Schmidt, and Artaria banded together with Stam and Lissitzky to form a new group, which they named ABC. Their proposed magazine was to bear the same name. But Lissitzky's affiliation with the group, despite his publishing expertise, presented a problem.

Lissitzky's arrival created an uncomfortable situation for the less radical Swiss who had joined or considered joining this new group—Werner Moser, Rudolf Steiger, and Max Ernst Haefeli. The small network of progressive Swiss architects that Stam encountered after arriving in Zurich in 1923 was not homogeneous and consisted of two factions: the radical pro-Communist activists from Basel—

Meyer, Wittwer, Artaria, Schmidt, and Roth (the last not a full-time Basel resident)—and the Zurich architects, Moser, Haefeli, and Steiger, who hailed from prominent establishment families. Werner Moser, very much the scion of one of Zurich's most honored architectural dynasties, was not yet prepared to battle for a pro-Communist cause. Max Ernst Haefeli, the son of the renowned Max Haefeli, president of the Swiss Werkbund, and Rudolf Steiger, son of Carl Steiger, an artist and experimental aviation designer, shared Moser's less radical loyalties. Furthermore, Steiger and Haefeli were also considerably younger than the others and were just completing their studies. Since they had not traveled or worked extensively, they were not prepared to channel their talents into any style as restrictive as ABC's. As a result, Steiger and Haefeli pulled back from the group at this time.

Werner Moser chose a far more unusual solution: during ABC's inaugural year, he migrated to the United States, not withdrawing or delaying his membership but becoming a corresponding member. Why the United States? While in Holland, the younger Moser had developed an intense interest in the work of Frank Lloyd Wright, one that the more radical Schmidt never shared. Wright was lionized by a large segment of the architectural community in Holland and reproductions of his designs were readily available there. While in Rotterdam, Moser studied Wright's designs and resolved to train under him in the United States—a surprising ambition for an ABC member.

Stam and Schmidt saw the United States as the nurturing core of capitalism and reactionary architecture. They had announced this on ABC's opening page.[9] Moser, however, believed that an admiration of the United States' technological advancements and architectural achievements was also in order. He viewed that country as a true home of modern architecture, where architects had liberated themselves from historicism and expressed structure and materials openly.

Like his father, Werner Moser believed in publicly promoting foreign architecture that he found inspirational. In an article in *Das Werk* entitled "Frank Lloyd Wright und amerikanische Architektur," he lauded America's architects for such accomplishments as utilitarian tall buildings, garages, silos, rail depots, and docks,[10] in addition to their emphasis on mass production and standardization, methods that were far less commonplace in Europe. In this article he also explained his admiration for Wright. Moser believed that European architects were novices in their understanding of contemporary technology. To overcome this deficiency they determined to prove their membership in the machine age by turning homes into sterile machinelike structures that had little connection with the natural environment. Admiration of nature was apparently an anachronism to these Europeans. Frank Lloyd Wright and many of his fellow American architects were not limited by such insecurities. Secure in their technical proficiency, they freely admitted to a love of nature and natural materials. In Wright's work Moser saw the perfect fusion of materials, structure, and nature, the ideal basis for a true modern architecture.

Moser was determined to incorporate this fusion into his own work. Already accustomed to studying abroad, the newly married Moser departed for Spring Green, Wisconsin, in early 1924 to live with Wright for almost two years. He worked in his atelier and designed, in tribute to his new master, such Wrightian structures as the Portland Cement Bungalow (Chicago) of 1924. Appropriately enough, this was a single-story bungalow of precast cement tiles with an overhanging pitched roof, prominent chimney, and expansive ground-level terraces. However, this work served only as a temporary foray on the part of Moser into a Wrightian idiom he would soon abandon. Moser soon realized that he was an ABC architect at heart after all, and he turned his talents to an ABC-type oeuvre within Wright's studio. Thereafter he designed structures that fused Wright's ideas and the ABC style.

Without Moser, Steiger, and Haefeli, ABC and its magazine became the sole domain of the radical Baslers, Stam, and Lissitzky. Since everyone who remained within the ABC circle was now openly pro-left, Stam and Lissitzky received sufficient support in declaring the new magazine a pro-Communist, pro-constructivist organ. *ABC Beiträge zum Bauen* commenced publication in the spring of 1924.

The ABC circle regarded the inaugural issue as a forum for the fulfillment of two obligations. The first was a vendetta against the *Schweizerische Bauzeitung*. This took the form of a black-rimmed obituary that blamed that magazine for the death of modern architecture in Switzerland. It appeared at the top of the second page of issue 1 and was signed by the bereft mourners—the ABC group.

2.6
Richard Neutra, Frank Lloyd
Wright, Erich Mendelsohn, and
Werner Moser at Taliesin,
Spring Green, Wisconsin,
1924.

Three

ABC Beiträge zum Bauen, 1924–1928: Guideline to a New Style

1

A Tribute to the Mentor

The ABC group's second obligation was to El Lissitzky. Indebted to him, the members intended to show their appreciation within the new magazine. *ABC Beiträge zum Bauen* was intended as the guideline to ABC constructivism. Eight issues of the publication appeared between 1924 and 1928, of which all but the first two developed aspects of ABC's new approach. Issues 1 and 2 of 1924 were decidedly different, as these were largely a tribute to Lissitzky.

The most obvious form of tribute was the adoption of the format that Lissitzky had created for *Veshch, Gegenstand, Objet*. Lissitzky had hoped that *Veshch* would serve as a model for future publications of the international network of small magazines that he so actively encouraged. *ABC's* editors fulfilled that wish. Ill and isolated in

Locarno, Lissitzky was not able to participate actively in the actual operations of *ABC*. He acted as the advisor to the official editors of the magazine, Mart Stam and Hans Schmidt, and to Emil Roth, the financial manager. Schmidt and Stam were also elected to design *ABC*. Having no previous experience in publication design, they looked to Lissitzky for guidance. Under his tutelage they adapted the format he had so successfully employed in *Veshch* and *G*. This approach was to remain a constant throughout *ABC*'s life span.

Veshch and *G* were remarkable publications. Their pages were characterized by striking contrasts and visual tensions the viewer was often unprepared for. Each page was an original amalgam of exaggerated type, unusual montage, bold illustration, the printer's rule, and novel text. Aside from content, it was layout that differentiated *Veshch* from *G*. *Veshch* tended to favor vertical sections (see figure 3.1) while *G* preferred frequent horizontal page divisions. Stam and Schmidt did their best to emulate both models, but without Lissitzky's personal talents the result was a weak imitation whose sources were obvious (figure 3.1). Following *Veshch*'s example, *ABC*'s title was relegated to the upper left and a brief editorial introduction followed on the upper right corner, with the printer's rule used in their delineation. Like *G*, the Swiss magazine selected a title from the alphabet and used a variety of typefaces throughout the issues. In keeping with precedents established in both *Veshch* and *G*, the editors here attempted to integrate montages, photographs, and original graphics with the text.

Despite these imitative efforts, *ABC*'s pages lacked Lissitzky's dramatic angles, scale variations, novel type arrangements, and certainly the surprise of the unexpected. The Swiss publication's illustrations rarely broke the boundaries of its double-column format. Unconventional type arrangements were missing and the typography was modest and fairly placid. As a result, *ABC* became predictable visually. Nonetheless, Stam and Schmidt's efforts did produce some positive and original results. Since they could not compete in Lissitz-

3.1

Opening page from *ABC Beiträge zum Bauen*, series 1, no. 3/4 (1925). Featured here is Mart Stam's "Beton" stamp and the article "Architektur Russlands" by Mart Stam and El Lissitzky. The article is prefaced by a woodcut of V. Tatlin's "Monument to the Third International," Moscow, 1919.

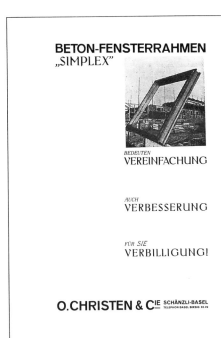

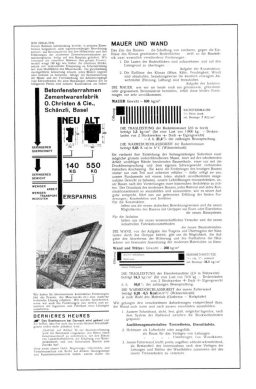

ky's arenas, they developed their own unique touches in order to grant *ABC* some graphic distinction.

Hans Schmidt often arranged *ABC*'s assorted entries within the magazine. His diaries list and itemize the articles for many issues, indicating that much of the responsibility for their publication was his. In addition, Schmidt also chose *ABC*'s typefaces. For example, the lettering for the *ABC* title and "Beiträge zum Bauen" did not recall those usually employed by Lissitzky. It was a type preferred by Schmidt and also used in a series of advertisements he created for the O. Christen & Cie. cement works in Basel in 1924 (figure 3.2). Three advertisements by Schmidt, not shown in *ABC*, made use of these typefaces. A more intricate version, a montage incorporating

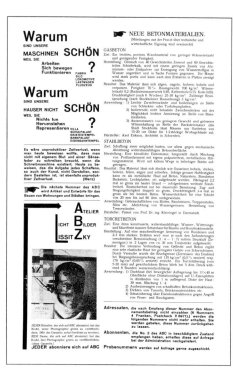

3.4
Page 8 from *ABC Beiträge zum Bauen*, series 1, no. 3/4 (1925), featuring "Warum schön" by Hans Schmidt and El Lissitzky's self-portrait montage "The Constructor," 1924.

a Christen frame and a typeface often used for *ABC* articles, was reproduced in *ABC* in 1925 (figure 3.3).

Schmidt also provided original graphic material. "Warum schön" was an example (figure 3.4). Although *ABC* did not specifically credit him for this item, two similar versions have been found in his unpublished papers (figure 3.5). It is not unlikely that Schmidt had been influenced by Lissitzky's preference for stepped formations.

Mart Stam's graphic abilities were showcased in *ABC* in a more limited and serendipitous manner. Stam liked to design block stamps and created one bearing his name that he used as a letterhead. *ABC Beiträge zum Bauen* featured other examples of this talent, such as the "Beton" stamp that appeared on the masthead of issue 3/4, 1925 (figure 3.1), and the small arrow at the top of issue 2 of 1924's first page.

In addition to design-related matters, *ABC*'s ideological support of Lissitzky and Asnova was quite pronounced in the first issues. The periodical's very first page featured the editorial "Russland," in which that country's avant-garde architects were lauded for their progressive new designs. "Moscau," the following editorial, was more specific. It acknowledged Asnova as a most noteworthy new group and offered *ABC*'s support of their efforts. Throughout later issues, *ABC* remained true to this allegiance and also featured previously unpublished designs by Simbirchev, Lamstov, and the atelier of Ladovsky as examples of Asnova work. These will be discussed in the next chapter.

ABC canonized Lissitzky's work in the early issues as well. The inaugural issue printed his seminal essay "Element und Erfindung" (Element and Invention) which gave a verbal rather than graphic account of the Asnova style. It described "naked constructions" comprised of suprematist forms and lauded these for their openness and their symbolic inferences. In addition, these constructions were enhanced by a network of bridges, elevators, towers, balloons, and illuminated billboards.[1]

ABC went on to feature additional articles and projects by Lissitzky, such as "Die Reklame" (Advertisement) and his montage "The Constructor" (see figure 3.4), which Lissitzky also referred to as his "Self-Portrait," and, in later issues, his Lenin Tribune and Proun Room.[2]

To further please its mentor, *ABC Beiträge zum Bauen* sought to become an affiliate of Lissitzky's network of pro-constructivist magazines as soon as it was established. The second issue featured the statement: "The ABC has 25 letters; whoever wishes to go beyond the first three, read and subscribe to: *Architectura, Contimporanue, MA, Manomètre, Mavo, Merz, Stavba, Zenit.*"[3] Later issues included a listing on each back cover of the 27 periodicals of the pro-constructivist network, including *Block, Disk, G, De Stijl,* and *Praesens.* The Swiss magazine also reprinted quotes and articles from publications sympathetic to, or edited by, Lissitzky. There was, for example, a lengthy quote from *Merz* in issue 3/4 as well as a brief excerpt from the Lissitzky article "Rad, Propeller und das Folgende" (Wheel, Propeller, and What Follows), which had appeared previously in *G.* And in 1926, Hans Richter's film stills from the same magazine.[4]

3.5

Page from an unpublished manuscript by Hans Schmidt, from the Hans Schmidt Archive of the Federal Institute of Technology, Zurich.

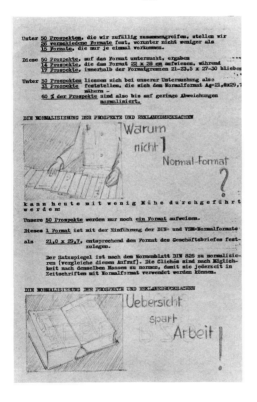

2

The ABC Position

It was only after *ABC*'s editors had discharged their obligations to Lissitzky that they finally focused on a definition of ABC constructivism. This long-awaited event occurred in issue 3/4 of 1925. In the article "Architektur Russlands" (Russia's Architecture), which appeared on the first page of that issue, the authors implied that there were aspects of Asnova's approach with which the ABC group could not agree. They called for, and subsequently presented, a new approach.

This new approach recalled Mart Stam's earlier appreciation of the Asnova style, in which he incorporated specific constructivist features into buildings that were conceived along functionalist lines. As later chapters will reveal, the ABC architects, like Stam, considered themselves functionalists. They recognized that modern building was a process in which pragmatic building methods, new materials, and economical mass-produced, standardized parts were fundamental. However, unlike some of their European contemporaries, they did not believe that functional buildings needed to be staid containers whose constructional process was a means to an end and not an integral part of the final design. ABC called for the blatant external expression of this process. In Asnova's projects the group found a vivid source of inspiration. Accordingly, the group elected to deemphasize the symbolic and formal aspects of Asnova constructivism and adapt the style's open manner of articulating materials, functions, structure, circulation systems, and innovative technological elements.

"Architektur Russlands" rejected formal and artistic concerns and favored an approach in which

structure is no longer enclosed, but open and skeletal and expressive of interior movement and parts. The building is an open construction revealing the interior functions on the exterior. In this manner clearly articulated interior functions become an integral part of the total composition. Its separate parts are then linked by a circulation system that includes elevators or cable railways, etc.[5]

"Das Volumen," an article that appeared in the following issue, reiterated these points: "We are prepared to accept into our designs those creations of technology—the cranes and various interior and exterior transport methods—so that we can create similar structures. . . . Over against the enclosed classical building stands the new architecture of lifts, cranes, transport and conveyor belts, and modern open construction."[6]

In order to reinforce its recognition of only the functionally viable features of Asnova works, *ABC* chose to publish Asnova projects in an unprecedented manner. Taking the projects Lissitzky had given *ABC* for publication, Stam and Schmidt presented them without their original titles. Instead, *ABC* took the liberty of creating new titles that excluded their theoretical raison d'être and emphasized only their functional properties. For example, issue 3/4 featured different views of a 1922 project by A. Arkin originally titled "Study in the Representation of Solid and Void: Tower for the Manufacture of Alkaline Solutions." *ABC*, however, offered only a simple caption that read: "Tower for the Production of Lye. . . . Elements: Cylinders, Stairs, Truss, and Ladders." Gruschenko's version of this same Atelier Ladovsky assignment was shown in issue 2 of 1924, where his "Study in the Representation of Solid and Void: Tower for the Manufacture of Alkaline Solutions" (see figure 1.4) was referred to only as a "tower for the production of lye." Under a version of Simbirchev's 1922 restaurant on a cliff, which was originally titled "Restaurant on a Cliff over a Lake: Exercise in the Representation of Formal Qualities of Mass and Equilibrium" (see figure 1.5), *ABC* simply stated: "Restaurant on a Cliff over a Lake: A construction demonstrating the technological possibilities of modern material and construction methods. A study of the function of stairs, platforms, and lifts."[7]

Other projects presented by *ABC* were similarly retitled. I. N. Lamstov's 1923 "Exercise in the Representation of Dynamism, Rhythm, etc." was shown as "Airport Model, Atelier Ladovsky, Moscow" in issue 6 of 1925. And Popova and Vesnin's "Sketch for the Struggle and Victory of the Soviets" was labeled "Flying Propaganda." Clearly, the project was valued for the "flying" or open manner in which the tensile elements of construction were displayed and for the bold incorporation of propaganda signs and placards into the scheme.[8] Once again, *ABC*'s architects wanted it made clear that they were interested only in those features of Asnova or Russian constructivism that were compatible with ABC ideology.

3 The Early ABC Style, 1924–1927

The ABC members did go on to develop a buildable style that was based on the principles outlined in the previous chapter, but this style was not successful until 1927. Between 1924 and 1927 the ABC group experimented with visionary ideas inspired by the Russian works Lissitzky had shown them. Although many of these works were not as farfetched as the Russian designs and may have been buildable, ABC's early efforts resulted in a paper architecture from which the mature ABC style first evolved in 1927.

The early examples of ABC constructivism owe their inspiration to Mart Stam and El Lissitzky. They date back to 1924–1925, the period during which Lissitzky, Stam, and other members first collaborated on ABC. Although Lissitzky had originally been invited only to consult for the magazine, he soon evolved into Stam's mentor on building design. It was Lissitzky who inspired Stam to graduate from his protoconstructivist style of 1922 into a more developed ABC constructivism. The Russian initially promoted the doctrinaire Asnova approach but soon realized that it was not acceptable to Stam, Roth, and the others. Consequently, he resolved to join Stam in creating a pragmatic hybrid constructivism by coauthoring the article "Architektur Russlands" with him. Lissitzky here compromised his position in order to keep the ABC members within the constructivist fold.

Mart Stam's projects were the trailblazers for the ABC movement. Under Lissitzky's influence he reshaped his 1922 ideas along more vibrant Russian lines, no longer insisting on the heavy-handed expression of structure seen at Königsberg or the rigid grid plan of Am Knie. Stam now adopted a new means of dramatizing structure and came to prefer plans that recalled the multidimensional, right-angled configurations seen in Lissitzky's Prouns. He also incorporated into his oeuvre such distinctive constructivist features as technological paraphernalia, exposed circulatory columns, open framework, and bold advertising. This change resulted in designs that were far more animated, lightweight, theatrical, and certainly more original than his earlier ones.

Stam was particularly influenced by the spatial arrangements of Lissitzky's Prouns. He sought to emulate in his buildings the manner in which these lightweight rectilinear forms dynamically bisected at one or several right angles. Two early school projects by Stam, the St. Wendel's Boys' Grammar School in Germany (1924) and the Thun Boys' Grammar School in Switzerland (1925), already display many of these features. Here individual functions, such as classrooms, recreational facilities, and circulation areas, are given separate pavilions, thereby establishing a precedent that would typify ABC work thereafter.

Following Stam's example, ABC's architects granted distinct volumes to distinct functions so that a building could be understood as a composite of functions. The individual pavilions or sections were then arranged in a series of interpenetrating right-angled formations, as they were in these schools. In obvious constructivist fashion, the building's parts were also linked and vivified by boldly segregated circulatory sections. This is particularly evident at the Thun school, where one entire wing is devoted to exaggerated staircases, ramps, and corridors. These designs and the many others discussed below were not published in *ABC Beiträge zum Bauen* due to limited space and to commitments by the architects to publish such works elsewhere. These schools, for example, were published in the Dutch architecture journal *Het Bouwbedrijf*.[9]

Stam's schools did not yet reveal his new manner of exposing structure, but his 1924 competition entry for the Cornavim rail station in Geneva did. Fortunately *ABC* published this work (figure 3.6). The Cornavim station contained numerous functions, and accordingly Stam designated distinct volumes for each within a large Proun-like composition that was skillfully knit to create a multidimensional image. It was also light in feeling, since the architect now called for all-glass crystalline pavilions that were anchored to the ground only by their interior structural members.

The exposition of the structural system is the core of the Cornavim station project. Resorting once again to the portal frame system presented in the Königsberg project, Stam now pulls the frames outside the perimeter of the building to emphasize their primary role within the overall design. The frames also lend drama, as the juxtaposition of such raw structure against the delicate walls creates a a very powerful contrast.

Further energizing the complex are such popular constructivist features as sharply angled exterior ramps and highly visible stairwells, which are strategically placed in prominent locations. A large advertisement for "Agfa Film" and an overscaled billboard announcing "Geneva Cornavim" add a sense of spectacle to the design. Col-

lectively these aspects made this competition entry one that would influence numerous ABC works to come.

Stam's constructivist visions grew in scale and impact with each passing year. Between 1924 and 1925, he and Emil Roth collaborated on an alternate version of Lissitzky's Wolkenbügel project for Moscow. Lissitzky created this well-known project while in Locarno (1924–1925). The Russian would show Stam and Roth plans for the project during their visits to his bedside. Knowing of Roth's training as a structural engineer, he asked his advice regarding the project's feasibility. Roth did not believe that Lissitzky's scheme, especially in the version that was shown to him, was structurally sound. Stam agreed with Roth and, with Roth's assistance, offered to draft a structurally viable alternative version.[10]

Lissitzky's version consisted of a series of staid T-shaped single-legged constructions that were structurally enclosed. Roth believed that such top-heavy structures needed more support. Accordingly, the Stam-Roth version presents a Wolkenbügel that rests on three aggressively angled supports per section (figure 3.7). The angled nature of these supports adds a dynamic animation that the original Lissitzky version clearly lacked. Furthermore, the Stam-Roth design seeks to expose structure and function completely. The giant supporting piers and elevator shafts are left unclad, startling the beholder. As a result, the revised Swiss version proves more explosive and visually exciting than the original Lissitzky version.

Not only were many Soviet works excessively grand, but they often prided themselves on their inclusion of unexpected transport methods. Stam's ambitious Rokin and Dam scheme of 1926 recalls both of these tendencies (figure 3.8). Rokin and Dam was part of a larger redevelopment scheme for an existing inner-city quarter of Amsterdam. This part was for the business district, which included office buildings, shops, restaurants, and theaters. Stam wanted his solution to stand out within this congested section of Rotterdam, and, had it been built, it would undoubtedly have done so. Here Stam resorted to his favored formula—the fusion of intersecting glazed Proun volumes, exposed structure, and memorable constructivist details. Rokin and Dam, however, surpassed any of Stam's previous complexes in

3.7
Alternative design to El Lissitzky's Wolkenbügel, 1924–1925, by Emil Roth and Mart Stam.

3.8
**Rokin and Dam project,
Amsterdam, 1926, by Mart
Stam. From *Internationale
Revue*, 1, no. 3 (1927),
pp. 86–88.**

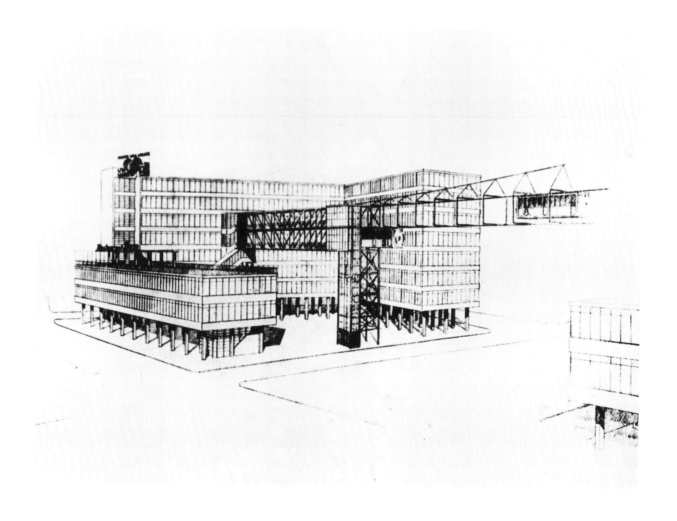

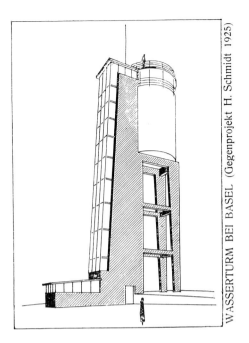

WASSERTURM BEI BASEL (Gegenprojekt H. Schmidt 1925)

3.9
Water Tower with Observation
Deck and Stair Tower project,
1925, by Hans Schmidt. From
ABC, series 2, no. 1 (1926),
p. 8.

its visionary outlook. Far more overpowering than Cornavim, Rokin and Dam's main buildings, which are actually stacked Proun pavilions, reach towering proportions. Furthermore, the entire complex is crowned by a flamboyant aerial tramway that is supported by a network of striking open-frame stations. As if more drama were necessary, a very large billboard sits atop the tallest building.

Rokin and Dam's design seems unrealistic because it is too theatrical and unconventional. The architect, however, did not have any misgivings about the feasibility of the project. Stam believed that this work, like all other ABC schemes, was realistic. He was therefore determined that his works be understood as functionally viable constructions. In *ABC Beiträge zum Bauen,* he presented his Cornavim entry with a lengthy text explaining the station's logical interior plan and its helpful position within Geneva's larger traffic plan. A similar approach was taken in the text presented with the Rokin and Dam plan. Rather than discussing the complex's obvious visual qualities, Stam focused on its clarity, honesty, and planning-related benefits.

Hans Schmidt followed the constructivist precedents Stam and the *ABC* magazine had established. In 1925, he designed a water tower that proved to be his most daring constructivist design. This was published in the magazine in 1926 (figure 3.9). Inspired by the Asnova works shown in the magazine, Schmidt chose to present his water tower as an amalgam of naked utilitarian parts that were combined for maximal visual impact. He even selected a title, "Water Tower with Observation Deck and Stair Tower," that recalled the titles *ABC* had used for the Arkin and Gruschenko towers for the production of lye.

Like these Asnova projects, this composition of frame, drum, and stairs is anything but a simple functional structure. Schmidt's water tower is a highly stylized composite that relies on formal and textural contrasts. It consists of an opaque cylinder (the drum) and a sequence of rectangular grids (the supporting frame) that contrast against a transparent, vertical circulation shaft. An observation deck and a flagpole are placed at the top of the water drum. These add yet another constructivist dimension; Russian constructivist buildings incorporated observation decks and flagpoles at times. In fact, the same *ABC* page that shows this water tower also features El Lissitzky's Speaker's (or Lenin) Tribune of 1926. Although the latter was a later work, it is shown to prove that Schmidt was inspired by the open frame, observation posts, and flags featured in ground-breaking Soviet works of the period.

Despite these formal points, *ABC* insisted on portraying Schmidt's tower as a functional alternative to traditional water towers. The publication's presentation included a diagram that emphasized the efficient inner workings of the technically sound, pared-down design, and then contrasted it against an existing traditional water tower that it deemed stylistically and technologically archaic.

Once he was no longer determined to imitate Wrightian houses, Werner Moser embraced ABC constructivism as well. In 1924, while Moser was working in Wright's atelier in Spring Green, Wisconsin, Wright was designing the headquarters for the National Life Insurance Company at Water Tower Square in Chicago. Moser had remained true to his promise to act as a corresponding ABC member and frequently exchanged letters with Schmidt and Stam. They also sent him copies of the *ABC* magazine. Impressed by the new constructivist ideas of his European colleagues, Moser decided to design an alternative constructivist version of the National Life Insurance building. It was published in *ABC* as "The office building on Pearcon Street, Chicago."

This office building was the first ABC-style skyscraper to appear in the magazine. It was not, however, the first Chicago skyscraper to be designed by an ABC member. In 1922, while in Berlin, Mart Stam had designed a towering Chicago Tribune competition entry. Stam's drawing was rather abstract and, aside from crystalline elevator shafts, did not illustrate structural particulars. Moser went on to produce a seemingly more viable skyscraper.

It was not Stam's or Wright's examples alone that prompted the younger Moser to create a skyscraper. America's skyscrapers in general fascinated him. Before settling in Wisconsin, he had traveled around parts of the United States and photographed numerous tall buildings during stages of their construction and in their completed form. Sometimes he sent these back to his ABC friends. For example, a photo of a half-completed Baltimore skyscraper and a sketch of a tall automated garage in Chicago shown in issues of *ABC* were submitted by Moser.[11] After admiring others' efforts, he finally chose to design his own skyscraper.

Indirectly, Wright was an influence. Werner Moser took the Wright building and reversed its allocation of spaces (figure 3.10). Wright had placed all offices within four towers that connected to a central service spine. Office spaces were the prominent elements while services were secondary and needed to be placed in visually unobtrusive places. Following ABC precedent, Moser changes this order by granting elevators and stairwells maximal prominence. These are housed in soaring glazed shafts that project from the glass-enclosed office slab. Lest there be any doubt of the constructivist intent, an enormous vertical marquee announces "National Life Insurance Company." To prove that this was a viable design, a sketch of the building's block constructional system was shown alongside the drawing of the building.

As impressive as Moser's design was, neither it nor any other ABC work of the period could compete with the oeuvre of Hannes Meyer and Hans Wittwer. Meyer and Wittwer established their Basel partnership in 1926. The partners infused early ABC constructivism with a dynamic energy rarely seen in Western European architecture. Of the two, Wittwer was the first to create notably constructivist designs. His 1925 Geneva Cornavim railroad station design called for a separation of functions into Proun-like interlocked sections (figure 3.11) and emphasis on connecting bridges and ramps. While structure may have defined Stam's Cornavim project, more overt elements such as dominating exterior bridges and ramps defined Wittwer's.

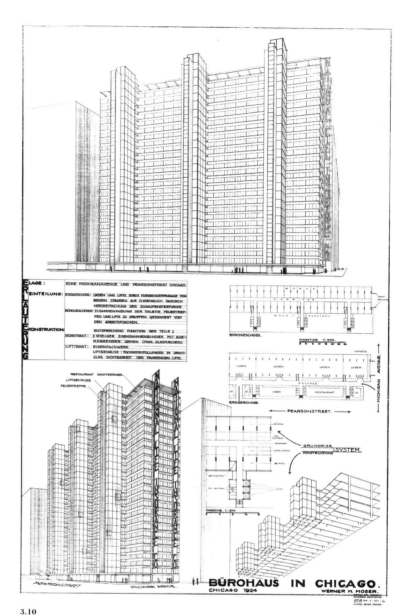

3.10
One version of the Bureauhaus
Pearconstreet project by
Werner Moser, Michigan
Boulevard, Chicago. A similar
drawing was published in *ABC*,
series 2, no. 3 (1926), p. 5.

3.11
Cornavim project, Geneva,
1925, by Hans Wittwer. Shown
in *ABC*, series 1, no. 6 (1925),
p. 2.

To contrast the two approaches, *ABC* showed this version opposite Stam's.

In 1926, Wittwer joined with his Basel friend Hannes Meyer to design the Petersschule for Girls in Basel, where their flair for theatrical elaboration revealed itself (figure 3.12). Their design was explosive, offering the least routine and most overstated interpretation of the ABC vocabulary. Stam's, Moser's, and even Schmidt's designs eventually came to follow a fairly predictable formula, but this design was anything but formulaic. The Petersschule was to remain a highly original presentation too unique to be imitated.

Unlike many contemporary ABC buildings, the Petersschule does not try to allude to lightness by emphasizing lightweight Proun-like volumes. Instead, it takes a far more daring and unexpected approach by actually implying flight. Indisputably defining this school is an enormous suspended ramp made of cables, trusses, and exposed frame that acts as a giant wing. Further eliciting awe from any viewer is the overwhelming scale of this ramp and its naked structure.

Wittwer and Meyer resort to unconventional means in their treatment of the main building as well. For example, they do not use glazed surfaces to distinguish circulatory sections and interior spaces. They expose these by turning the building inside out and placing functional and circulatory parts outside the building. A staircase ascends the exterior of the building while a normally enclosed roof area is shown framed, but without walls. Further stressing externalization is the

3.12
**Petersschule project, Basel,
1926, by Hans Wittwer and
Hannes Meyer. Shown in**
Bauhaus, **2 (Dessau, 1927),
p. 5.**

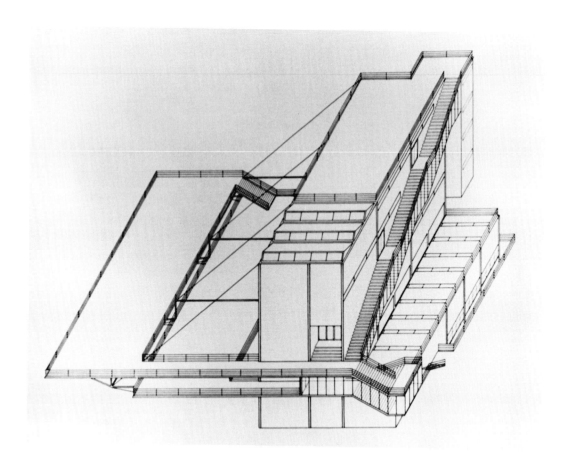

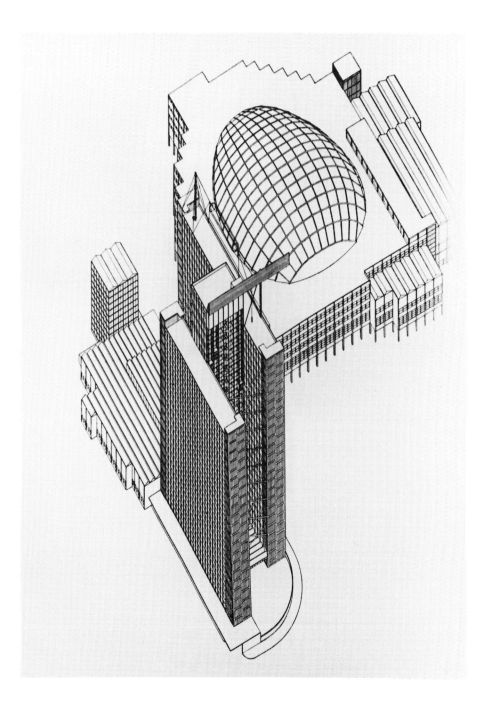

giant ramp, which is intended as a play and assembly area. Only those areas that require privacy and protection from the elements at all times—the classrooms, offices, and gymnasium—remain indoors. These areas receive natural light from skylights and large ribbon windows on the east facade.

With the Petersschule, Meyer and Wittwer succeeded in expanding the stylistic boundaries of ABC constructivism. Not even this building, however, prepares one for the scale of their League of Nations project for Geneva (1926–1927; figure 3.13). The League of Nations is a startling collage of the richest vocabulary seen in any ABC work to date. This complex, an amalgam of commanding skyscrapers, a colossal assembly hall, and assorted low-rise pavilions, is cohesive despite divergences in scale, form, and size. Its plan includes rectangular, square, elliptical, circular, and triangular forms, in scales that range from the ordinary to the boundlessly monumental and heights that move from the low-rise to the soaringly vertical. The masterful unification of such opposites results in a powerful whole.

Two features in particular unify this vision. According to Meyer, the specific goal of the League of Nations was to "eliminate the underhanded methods of obsolete secret diplomacy . . . in an open assembly of the representatives of all member nations . . . served by the will to attain truth."[12] The architects translated "truth" to mean a vigorous exposition of function and structure throughout the complex. Wittwer and Meyer's efforts resulted in a crystalline vision vivified by such forceful structural elements as X bracings.

Further unifying the complex is a profound sense of lightness. Despite their size, the buildings of the League of Nations never appear to be massive. Instead they appear surprisingly lightweight, as all the main buildings remain deliberately above ground. The auditorium's ground floor rests on a colonnade of pilotis while the skyscraper towers sit on a low curved section. Only the low-rise pavilions appear bound to earth, since they touch the soil. Many of Wittwer and Meyer's drawings of this project are from a bird's-eye perspective, thereby reinforcing a floating sensation. More than any large-scale ABC design, the League of Nations project proves that neither structural realities nor complicated agendas could prevent ABC's visionaries from believing that buildings could give the illusion of defying gravity.

Lest one doubt the constructivist bias here, a huge screen and a rising network of antennae, cables, and poles embellish this Herculean effort. And yet, despite the extremities of his design, Hannes Meyer insisted that the League of Nations was designed only with "purpose in mind" and not as an "exercise in stylistic composition."[13] Naturally, the written proposals that accompanied the Petersschule and the League of Nations further focused on the projects' functional correctness and structural viability.

Four

The Dream Becomes a Reality, 1927–1931

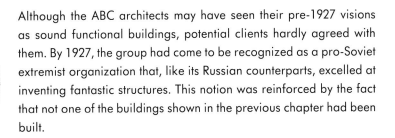

1

1927: A Change in Focus, an Expansion of Ranks

Although the ABC architects may have seen their pre-1927 visions as sound functional buildings, potential clients hardly agreed with them. By 1927, the group had come to be recognized as a pro-Soviet extremist organization that, like its Russian counterparts, excelled at inventing fantastic structures. This notion was reinforced by the fact that not one of the buildings shown in the previous chapter had been built.

Eager to build, the members recognized that they had to change their outlook if they were to become practicing architects. In 1927 they realized that their alliance with Lissitzky and Asnova was the core of their problem, steering them in a direction that deterred Western clients. Stam, Schmidt, and their colleagues saw only one solution. ABC had to distance itself from all Russian architects and align itself with more acceptable factions within the European avant-garde. This did not prove to be difficult, since Lissitzky had returned to the USSR in 1925.

ABC Beiträge zum Bauen clearly documented this change of heart. There is a marked difference between the content of the issues prior to 1927 and the comprehensive final issue dated 1927–1928. In all the issues but the last there had been at least one article, photograph, or project by a Russian. In the final issue, not only were these former friends ignored but they were openly refuted.

The last page of the publication featured the article "Kunst" (Art). In *Veshch, Gegenstand, Objet,* El Lissitzky had made it clear that constructivism was an ecumenical movement that encompassed painting, sculpture, and other branches of the arts. Accordingly, he published examples of them all in his periodicals, and the network of small constructivist magazines followed suit. *ABC,* in order to be recognized as a true constructivist publication, had conformed to this prescription by featuring examples of constructivist-inspired sculpture, advertising, painting, film, and montage. "Kunst" now invalidated this approach, stating that art had deteriorated into kitsch. The spirit of invention that seemed so promising at an earlier time had never come to true fruition; art had lost its spirit and originality and no longer merited canonization. With these words *ABC* absolved itself of its multicultural focus and pointedly implied disappointment in Lissitzky. After all, "Element and Invention," Lissitzky's optimistic ode to design, had been the most memorable article within *ABC*'s inaugural issue.[1]

ABC's new position was further documented throughout the final issue. Shown there were drawings by Stam for the Weissenhof Siedlung in Stuttgart and preliminary plans for the Schorenmatten Colony in Basel by Schmidt and Artaria. The Weissenhof Siedlung was sponsored by the German Werkbund and the Schorenmatten Colony was inspired by the policies of the Swiss Werkbund. Up until this time,

ABC had aligned itself only with Asnova. Now it consciously changed direction and forged bonds with acknowledged European organizations whose members worked and built.

By 1927 all Swiss ABC members, with the exceptions of Meyer and Wittwer who had migrated to Germany, were active members of the Swiss Werkbund (SWB). As the Swiss Werkbund's platform was more moderate than ABC's, the ABC group adopted a more tolerant stance in order to facilitate the union. This newfound tolerance resulted in an expansion of ABC's ranks. In 1924, ABC's pro-Russian position had alienated Max Ernst Haefeli and Rudolf Steiger. Instead of participating in ABC's activities they devoted their time to the Werkbund. Once ABC's Swiss members had divorced themselves from Lissitzky and modified their point of view, Steiger and Haefeli reaffiliated themselves with the group. Another factor that promoted this reunion was Werner Moser's return from the United States in 1926. Once in Zurich, Moser rejoined his ABC colleagues and thereafter the Werkbund. Haefeli and Steiger were eager to join their good friend in as many ventures as possible, including ABC.

It was through the Werkbund that the members became increasingly aware of a young man many had known for several years, Karl Egender. Born in the town of Burzweiler, Alsace, in 1897, he apprenticed as a draftsman in the office of Gebrüder Wassner, studied with Paul Bonatz in Stuttgart in 1920, and one year later came to Zurich. There he met and impressed Karl Moser. Moser introduced him to his son Werner and to members of his ETH circle. Hans Schmidt was one of Egender's outspoken admirers and the men became friends. In 1922, Egender formed a partnership with Adolf Steger that was to last through 1932.

Karl Egender began a unique affiliation with the ABC group during 1927. He took no part in any of the group's ideological decisions, but became an associate who adopted the ABC approach. Egender's understanding of the ABC idiom was extraordinary. Strandbad Kusnacht, a private bathing club in Zurich that was designed and built

4.1
**Strandbad Kusnacht, Zurich,
1928–1929, by Karl Egender
and Adolf Steger. Current
photo, © 1992 Walter Mair.**

between 1928 and 1929, proves this unequivocally (figure 4.1). Whether or not he was influenced by Simbirchev's Restaurant on a Cliff or not, the restaurant portion of this club captures the Russian project's impact. In Strandbad Kusnacht, Egender created a series of seemingly cantilevered stepped horizontal planes, crowned by a dynamically angled roof, that forcefully jut out to the lake. All the areas in between the slabs are either glass-enclosed or—the ultimate statement in dematerialization—completely open to the elements. The forceful thrust of Egender's restaurant has little in common with typical Swiss bathing clubs of the period and everything in common with the ideals of ABC.

Egender's marginal role within ABC may have resulted from his relationship with Steger. After their partnership ended, Egender suddenly assumed a far more vocal and active role in ABC. In 1932, he also joined CIAM, which at that time had become the major source of support for the ABC group. The other ABC members had joined CIAM in 1928.

Thus, by 1927 the ABC roster was complete. Years later, when Hans Schmidt was asked to cite ABC's Swiss members, he named Werner Moser, Max Ernst Haefeli, Rudolf Steiger, Emil Roth, Karl Egender, Hans Schmidt, Paul Artaria, Hans Wittwer, and Hannes Meyer.[2] With El Lissitzky back in the USSR and its revised membership in full force, ABC moved toward the realization of its original goal, which was to build constructivist-style functional buildings.

In addition to crippling financial problems, it was this revised attitude that finally ended their magazine's run with the 1927–1928 issue. The pro-Soviet image that *ABC Beiträge zum Bauen* had perpetuated was no longer desirable. Furthermore, the members' meteoric successes between 1927 and 1928 no longer afforded them sufficient time to work on the magazine.

2

ABC and the Swiss and German Werkbunds, 1927–1931

By the late 1920s the ABC group had transformed itself into a network of influential working architects. Fortunate timing facilitated this sudden about-face. ABC chose to affiliate itself with the German Werkbund just as the Weimar government was preparing to subsidize large-scale modern housing developments, and with the Swiss Werkbund at exactly the time when the latter more fully embraced modernism. These two organizations gave ABC members the early commissions that paved the way for their rise within Europe's architectural community.

In 1927, the Swiss Werkbund truly committed itself to modernism. Founded by Max Haefeli (senior) in 1915 and directed by Alfred Altherr, its reputation had rested since 1918 on "Die Wohnung" (The

Home) exhibitions at the Kunstgewerbemuseum in Zurich, a branch of the Werkbund. But prior to 1927, the architecture featured in these shows could hardly be described as radical. That situation changed rapidly after an invitation was extended to the Swiss Werkbund by the German Werkbund to participate in the Weissenhof Siedlung, a model housing development in Stuttgart that opened in the summer of 1927.

The German government agreed to fund this development, thereby establishing, though only temporarily, a precedent for governmental subsidizing of experimental or progressive housing in that country. As a result of such patronage, Weimar Germany became one of the most notable patrons of modern architecture in this century. Prompting this generosity was the Weimar Republic's determination to rebuild itself after World War I. Optimistically the republic began to underwrite the construction of schools, housing, and municipal buildings in 1924. Given Weimar's socialist predisposition, many of these commissions went to radical leftist architects. Weimar's policy of subsidizing building reached its pinnacle in 1927 with the establishment of the Reichsforschungsgesellschaft für Wirtschaftlichkeit im Bau und Wohnungswesen (RFG). It was the aim of this agency to fund such new and experimental low-cost housing programs as the Weissenhof Siedlung.

The German Werkbund intended the Weissenhof Siedlung to be a historic event that would establish new international standards in architecture. Architects of many nationalities were invited to participate, including the Swiss. Friedrich T. Gubler, the secretary of the Werkbund, requested that the director of the Swiss Werkbund select a group to design some of the interiors. Hans Schmidt, Paul Artaria, Werner Moser, Karl Egender, Rudolf Steiger, and Max Ernst Haefeli were among the members chosen for this honor. Haefeli was designated as the group's leader.

The chosen architects were assigned the interiors of the large Mies van der Rohe building on the Weissenhof campus. Haefeli designed original furnishings for the building; Schmidt drafted the floor plans. Schmidt's plans already typified his subsequent work, in that they featured layouts based on a system in which specific functions were assigned standardized dimensions. The Weissenhof interiors marked the first time that members of the newly expanded ABC group collaborated on a project.

Mart Stam was invited to participate in the Weissenhof Siedlung as well. Stam was accorded a distinction not granted to any of his Swiss colleagues: he was asked to design a small block of three apartments in his own right. He recognized this as an opportunity to establish precedents that could influence future ABC mass housing designs. Stam understood that Weissenhof required a specific agenda of its own, one that had little in common with ABC's flamboyant earlier works. Since the underlying concerns of mass housing were economy and simplicity, Stam created a subdued and economical manner of constructivist expression that better suited this type of development.

Stam's Weissenhof entry was a study in minimal presentation and jarring embellishment (figures 4.2 and 4.3 and plate 1). True to the ABC credo, he intended that the three apartments utilize as many mass-produced parts as possible. Consequently, he designed a large rectangular volume to house three units whose bare facades were punctuated by standardized windows and doors.

To prevent monotony, he vivified the exteriors with ABC-inspired details. As ABC constructivism externalized circulatory parts and structural members, Stam chose to emphasize the same features at Weissenhof, but in a novel and less costly way. To Stam this meant drawing attention to these features via a simple but shocking presentation. He chose to allude to structure by emphasizing such select members as metal railings, featured in as harsh a manner as possible. Entry into any of his Weissenhof apartments from the street requires one to ascend a raw staircase of undisguised poured concrete and spartan industrial metal railing. Then one must make a

4.2
**Weissenhof Siedlung
apartments, Stuttgart, 1927, by
Mart Stam, showing the framed
"outdoor room." Archival
photo.**

ght-angle turn onto a narrow bridge section before the front door can be reached. More is in store at the rear of the house. Direct entry to the second floor from the ground requires one to climb a spiral metal staircase that leads to a bridge. This bridge is longer, made of metal, and utilizes the same open railing as on the first floor—a railing that could be dangerous to young children and the elderly.

The building's plan and constructional system rely on the economical use of space and, according to Stam, on functional, low-cost construction methods. Stam uses a metal skeleton, precast concrete slab floors, and non-load-bearing external walls of concrete block. These walls allow windows to be set flush into exterior walls for maximal volumetric effect. The floor plans feature an open dining-living space rather than a series of smaller rooms on the ground floor, and a space-efficient arrangement of bedrooms on the upper floor. ABC's architects were much impressed. Virtually all mass housing schemes by Schmidt, Artaria, and Haefeli echoed Weissenhof's floor plans, and its constructional system was widely adopted by ABC members for homes and mass housing developments.

Another feature placed these apartments within the mainstream of ABC constructivism. ABC buildings expressed interior functions externally. Early ABC projects covered themselves in glass to achieve this goal; since this was a very expensive method of exposure, Stam devised a simpler and less costly one for Weissenhof. He created an "exterior room"—an outdoor extension of the house that was framed and sometimes included window frames and a door, but had no walls or roof. Meyer and Wittwer had already created such a space atop the Petersschule, where the roof was enclosed by a network of metal frames, giving the impression of a framed room with invisible walls. At Weissenhof, Stam turned the second-story terrace into an outdoor room by means of a wall of window frames and a door that leads to the circular staircase. In his later residential work, Stam continued to feature outdoor rooms and exposed circulatory areas. His fellow ABC architects followed suit; after 1927, most ABC housing included outdoor stairwells as well as open rooms in the form of rooftop terraces, porches, and ground-level patios.

The Weissenhof building was also the first built ABC structure to be painted a color. Color played an important role in Russian constructivism: it was used for theatrical or allegorical purposes by members of the Asnova group, vivifying Vladimir Krinsky's "Project for the ARKOS Society, Moscow" (1924); and many of Lissitzky's designs, including the Prouns and an architectural scheme for a yacht club in the Gorky Park of Rest and Culture (1925), were defined in color. Like their Russian contemporaries, ABC's architects sometimes employed color to dramatize the exteriors or interiors of their buildings. As early as 1919, Hannes Meyer, already an admirer of postrevolutionary Soviet art, suggested that his Freidorf colony be painted a political red. For the front facades of the Weissenhof apartments Stam selected a striking shade of light blue, a color that certainly set them apart from their white Weissenhof neighbors. ABC's architects soon followed Stam's example and incorporated color into their designs in unexpected ways.

4.3
Weissenhof Siedlung apartments, Stuttgart, 1927, by Mart Stam. Archival photo.

Stam was also asked to design the interiors of his dwellings. Seeing this as the opportunity for his first *Gesamtkunstwerk,* he designed his own original furniture. Among the chairs included was his now famous tubular steel chair, often said to be the first of its genre. In its final issue, *ABC Beiträge zum Bauen* featured his article "Fort mit den Möbelkünstlern! Wohnhäuser Stuttgart 1927," which explained that his spartan interior plans were intended for the new working-class family in which both husband and wife worked. Stam's distinctive interiors and their minimal furniture were shown in the accompanying illustrations.[3]

The Weissenhof apartments established numerous precedents that not only Stam but the other ABC members would follow for years to come. Stam's use of color, select industrial imagery, exterior rooms, and spartan interiors set in motion a wave of variations that came to typify low-cost residential ABC buildings in Germany and Switzerland.

The overall success of the Weissenhof Siedlung had a marked impact on the Swiss Werkbund. Its members felt that the time had come to show the international architectural community that Switzerland was not a cultural backwater but a nation capable of producing remarkable modern architecture. Thus the Swiss organization decided to construct its own model housing exhibition, conceived along Weissenhof lines, to be included in the Zurich Kunstgewerbemuseum's "Das Heim" exhibition of 1928. A site was selected on the Wasserwerkstrasse parallel to the Limmat River, and a competition for the final design was announced. Greatly inspired by Stam's Stuttgart houses, Max Ernst Haefeli submitted an entry that had much in common with them. Haefeli won and the houses were built in time for the show.

Max Ernst Haefeli's Wasserwerkstrasse flats, known as the Rotachhäuser, were among the earliest built ABC homes in Switzerland and are still in use today (figure 4.4). Following Stam's example, they too are a complex of three flat-roofed connected duplexes punctuated by plain standardized windows. They differ from the Stam version in that they are more three-dimensional, as the units are placed in staggered formation and their silhouettes are broken by porches.

ABC's spirit certainly manifests itself in the details. Originally the Rotach buildings were separated from the street by a small ravine. Three simple ABC-style bridges, whose railings consisted of panels of mesh metal fencing, connected the Rotachhäuser to the street—a most ungainly but visually striking way to enter one's home. All the outdoor staircases and porches are still enclosed by this unattractive railing, giving an unduly severe image to the entire complex's exterior. There was also an effort to create outdoor rooms, including ground-level patios, porches, and roof-level terraces. The latter were defined by vertical and horizontal poles that framed out the dimensions of a room (figure 4.5).

Mart Stam's influence manifests itself at the Rotachhäuser in yet another fashion. At the Weissenhof Siedlung, Stam had juxtaposed austere imagery against lighthearted color. Haefeli added color to these stern buildings as well, but not on their exteriors. His stoic facades hardly prepare one for the indoor explosion of color. Radiant yellows, greens, and oranges cover many walls. Light and spaciousness characterize the interior as well. Glass panels rather than masonry walls enclose such spaces as kitchens (figure 4.6), while the central staircase is placed within a generous open space. The unexpected optimism of these interiors proved that Haefeli, like Stam, had mastered the ability to surprise his audience with unexpected contrasts.

Haefeli's flats received widespread publicity in Switzerland and created an interest in such housing. This new spirit inspired the Swiss Werkbund and some governmental agencies to fund ABC-inspired low-income housing developments in Basel and Zurich. Among these was the Schorenmatten Colony in Basel, a commission that was given to Hans Schmidt and Paul Artaria (figure 4.7).

Schorenmatten was a cooperative for low-income residents planned under the auspices of the architect August Kunzel. However, Artaria and Schmidt were its active designers. Designed between 1927 and 1928 and built in 1929, Schorenmatten consisted of 63 flats under the name of Lange Erlen that were subsidized by the city of Basel and 29 under the name Rüttibrunnen that were not. Since World War II fortunately did not leave Switzerland in ruins, these flats, like virtually all the Swiss buildings that will be discussed, remained and are still inhabited to date.

ABC Beiträge zum Bauen's final issue featured Schmidt's articles "Typengrundrisse" and "Wohnkolonie."[4] Both discussed Schorenmatten, although not by name. The published site plan is identical to that of the Basel colony. The subtitle for the "Wohnkolonie" is "For families with many children," a description by which Schorenmatten was also known in the magazine.

There are similarities between Schmidt's drawings and Stam's earlier model. Like Stam, Schmidt sought to create extremely simple and functional interior plans. In fact, according to this article he went so far as to develop a standardized approach to interior planning based on the exact amount of space a function warranted. The exterior designs shown in the *ABC* magazine feature rectilinear blocks of flats with simple arrangements of windows, outdoor corridors, and spartan exterior staircases. Artaria and Schmidt's final designs were even simpler that those shown in *ABC*, featuring the most minimal arrangement of windows and doors ever seen in any ABC building. These flats did not need ominous industrial elements to lend them austerity—that quality was inherent in the design itself.

In 1929, the Swiss Werkbund agreed to underwrite a far more expansive housing exhibition. This exhibition, which was to be Switzerland's version of Weissenhof, was named the WOBA (Wohnung Genossenschaft Ausstellung) Eglisee. It was sited in Basel adjacent

to the Schorenmatten colony. Organized and funded in 1929, it opened to the public in 1930. Like the exhibition that had inspired it, WOBA Eglisee intended to promote avant-garde housing prototypes. The essential differences between the WOBA and Weissenhof exhibitions were that the Basel show was limited to Swiss architects and all the prototypes displayed in it were intended for modest-income residents only. (The German exhibition included architects of many nationalities, and some of the houses shown, such as Le Corbusier's two entries, hardly qualified as models for working-class families.) Twenty-two of Switzerland's leading modernists were invited to participate, including Schmidt, Artaria, Moser, Roth, and Egender. All the models together occupied 13 blocks. ABC's approach clearly shaped this exhibition. In keeping with ABC standards, the participating architects were requested to produce low-cost buildings that made use of mass-produced standardized parts. Many of the resulting designs were exceptionally reductive and straightforward. Today, many are still in use and are painted in

4.7
Schorenmatten Colony, Basel,
1927–1929, by Paul Artaria
and Hans Schmidt. Current
photo, © 1992 Walter Mair.

pastel hues; it is not possible to ascertain if these were in fact the original colors.

Hans Schmidt and Paul Artaria were unquestionably the dominating presences at the WOBA exhibition. Because of their successful execution of the adjoining Schorenmatten, they were treated as reigning experts and given the largest commission, sixteen attached single-family townhouses. Like those in Schorenmatten, these consisted of minimally detailed longitudinal blocks distinguished mainly by simple arrangements of row windows and doors. While Schmidt and Artaria may have had the largest entry, it was Werner Moser and Emil Roth's block that best represented the ABC idiom (figure 4.8). Closely following Mart Stam's Weissenhof example, their building featured industrial-style stairs and railings set at a right angle to small entry ramps. The row of flats is otherwise unadorned and punctuated only by a rigid arrangement of windows and doors set

4.8
WOBA Eglisee Colony, Basel, 1929–1930. Flats by Emil Roth and Werner Moser. Current photo, © 1992 Walter Mair.

flush into the walls. The block is currently painted a tropical light green.

Oddly enough, one of the finest ABC-style examples was attributed to someone outside the group. Kellermüller and Hofmann of Basel submitted a design highly reminiscent of Hans Schmidt's 1927 three-story Wohnkolonie project that had appeared in *ABC*. The version by Kellermüller and Hofmann called for a very similar arrangement of windows and outdoor corridors. As in the Schmidt version, the barely visible pillars, thin overhanging roof, and minimal railing lent a graceful lightness to what might otherwise be an unduly austere facade.

WOBA Eglisee was in turn the inspiration for an even larger Swiss Werkbund colony, Neubühl (figure 4.9). WOBA Eglisee was only intended as a temporary exhibition, although it was never demol-

4.9
Neubühl Colony, Zurich,
1930–1932. Archival photo by
Swissair-Photo A.G.

ished. Neubühl was to be a permanent large-scale development sited on the mountainous slopes three miles outside of Zurich, overlooking the city's lake, the Zürichsee. The Werkbund awarded this choice commission to those architects who had proven themselves to be most influential at WOBA, the ABC members. Neubühl was designed and built between 1930 and 1932 by Hans Schmidt, Paul Artaria, Werner Moser, Emil Roth, Max Ernst Haefeli, Rudolf Steiger, and Steiger's then partner, Carl Hubacher. Since Zurich real estate was too costly to permit a low-income development, it was planned as a middle-income cooperative.

From the outset the architects decided that Neubühl would offer several standardized housing types. These would be sited within a functional scheme that best accommodated traffic patterns, land contours, and maximal exposure to light and air. The approach they chose was based on a scheme for a similar site that Emil Roth had discussed in his 1925 ABC article "Gelände und Bebauung am Zürichsee." Roth had described a development of rows of low-rise attached houses that ascended the Zürichsee's banks in stepped formation, laid out parallel to the lake and in accordance with the contours of the mountainous terrain. Roth believed that such a scheme permitted maximal exposure to light and unobstructed views of the lake. In the article, he stipulated that the houses should be limited to only several types and that their floor plans should address essential needs in a compact manner. His scheme also focused on the project's connection to Zurich's existing road network. He called for an internal system of streets, placed at right angles to the housing rows and connected to existing roads and local tram lines.[5]

The Neubühl Colony's 195 units ranged from one- to six-room layouts. Buildings were constructed according to a system that had been described in another ABC article, "Technische und wirtschaftliche Resultate eines Wohnhausbaues" by Hans Schmidt, in which he detailed the constructional system he had used for his Colnaghi House: a steel skeleton with exterior walls of concrete block sheathed in an outer layer of concrete.[6]

Stylistically, the housing types at Neubühl ranged from adaptations of earlier Werkbund versions to originals. Some of the simpler blocks certainly echoed WOBA Eglisee. For example, Kellermüller and Hofmann's multistory terraced building was closely imitated in four-story form here. Simpler rows echoed Roth and Moser's spartan WOBA Eglisee homes, featuring right-angled stairs with industrial railings at entrances and the usual regimen of simple windows spread across planar facades. In keeping with ABC precedent, other Neubühl housing types emphasized stairwell sections and terraces.

Neubühl also offered some unexpected rewards. Among them were housing rows that far surpassed the prevailing ABC types in their sculptural quality (figure 4.10). In these rows each unit was treated as part of a larger serial progression whose cuboid planes and volumes pushed and pulled in a manner reminiscent of cubist sculpture or De Stijl constructions. This was particularly evident in the multidimensional roof levels. As a result of rows such as these and the overall excellence of its design, Neubühl has come to be regarded as one of the most noteworthy examples of Swiss mass housing of this century.

One more example by Mart Stam of outstanding low-income mass housing must be included in this overview. After the Weissenhof Siedlung, Stam became increasingly close to a new friend, the German architect Ernst May. This proved to be a most fortuitous friendship, since May was in charge of the building program of the city of Frankfurt am Main and was thus one of the most powerful figures within Germany's extensive building program. Ludwig Landmann, Frankfurt's mayor, a Socialist and advocate of mass communal housing, had appointed May, a leftist, to direct all public housing projects in 1925. Under May's direction over 15,000 housing units were built over the next five years. Many were within such exemplary *Siedlungen* as Römerstadt and Praunheim.

One of the projects on May's agenda was the 800-unit Hellerhof colony (figure 4.11). Most impressed by Stam's Weissenhof solution,

4.10
Neubühl Colony, Zurich,
1930–1932. Current photo,
© 1992 Walter Mair.

4.11
Hellerhof, Frankfurt am Main,
1928, by Mart Stam. Current
photo, © 1992 Walter Mair.

he invited Stam to Frankfurt and asked him to design and supervise the construction of this *Siedlung*. The expansive Hellerhof complex was designed and built in 1928 and is still in use today. Here garden facades often have ample terraces and generous windows. Street facades are another matter; Stam's multistory buildings bear a striking resemblance to the barracks-like two-story housing blocks Schmidt and Artaria designed for Schorenmatten (see figure 4.7). Regardless of the number of stories involved, these unfriendly facades are animated only by the tension between slashes of horizontal windows and narrow vertical doors. There is one additional element that adds dimensionality, a thin projecting plane over doorways that Stam had first used at Weissenhof on the street facade. As might be expected, prominent exterior stairwells appear at the sides of the individual multistory blocks. These stairwells also echo the proposal shown in the *ABC* magazine, as they were expanded versions of the types proposed for Schorenmatten.

3

Schmidt, Artaria, Moser, and Haefeli: Residences, 1927–1931

These public housing projects do not illustrate ABC residential design in its most developed form. Fortunately, ABC members accepted private residential commissions during this time that allowed them to develop more fully the constructivist approach they had previously formulated. The villas of Hans Schmidt, Paul Artaria, Werner Moser, and Max Ernst Haefeli exemplify how ABC houses evolved into dynamic sculptural entities once economic and social constraints were removed. These villas fused some of the points Stam had stressed at Weissenhof with features that recalled the more theatrical and dynamic aspects of early ABC constructivism.

For example, the floor plans of many of the residences, rather than being simple rectilinear volumes, once again remind one of Lissitz-

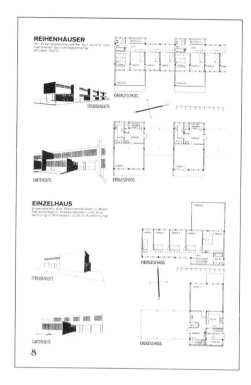

REIHENHÄUSER
für Eisenskelettbauweise auf Grund normalisierter Grundrisselemente
(Projekt 1927)

OBERGESCHOSS

STRASSENSEITE

GARTENSEITE

ERDGESCHOSS

EINZELHAUS
Eisenskelett aus Stahlrohrstützen u. Breitflanschträgern, Massivdecken und Ausfachung in Bimsbeton (z.Zt.in Ausführung)

STRASSENSEITE

OBERGESCHOSS

GARTENSEITE

ERDGESCHOSS

8

4.12
Reihenhäuser (row house) and
Einzelhaus (single-family house)
by Paul Artaria and Hans
Schmidt, as shown in *ABC*,
series 2, no. 4 (1927–1928),
p. 8.

ky's Prouns. Free to expand their visions, the architects presented their houses not as singular volumes but, in true ABC fashion, as compounds of interlocking multidimensional forms. Not unexpectedly, these rectangular compounds often placed marked emphasis on outdoor spaces and circulatory passages as well. In keeping with ABC's utilitarian spirit, industrial imagery featured prominently, often in the form of railings. Despite such similarities, the ABC villas had little in common with ABC's austere mass housing prototypes. They were elegant and unusually animated structures that were quite original for their time.

Two drawings in *ABC*'s last issue illustrate this more developed approach. Residential designs by Artaria and Schmidt, under the headings "Reihenhäuser 1927" and "Einzelhaus 1927," are versions of a multifamily row house complex and a single-family home (figure 4.12). Although the *ABC* titles are not specific, the former was actually the Maisonette-Laubeganghaus project that was shown at the "Heim und Technik" (Home and Technology) exhibition in Munich in 1928, and the latter an early prototype of the Schaeffer House (1928) in Rhien, an exclusive Basel suburb. These buildings are studies in the interpenetration of volumes.

After 1927, Artaria and Schmidt's homes continued to grow in size and complexity, from the relatively simple plan of the Schaeffer House, which relied on a single right-angled juncture, to larger formations based on multiple interlocking volumes. As their buildings developed, individual parts and sections gained definition, becoming distinct sections within multidimensional compositions. The 1927–1928 Colnaghi House in Rhien, Switzerland, which was shown in *ABC*, offers a full-scale exploration of this approach (figures 4.13 and 4.14). Artaria and Schmidt's most intricate villa, its three sections knit together on a central axis to form a dynamic cubist configuration. Each facade is unique and is enriched by the contrast of open and closed parts within each particular volume.

Artaria and Schmidt's innovative cubist imagery was evident in other buildings as well. For example, the staccato motion of cubelike porches across the street facade of their 1928 Home for Unwed Mothers in Basel (figure 4.15) results in a rhythmic push-pull effect commonly associated with the canvases of Braque or Mondrian, but not with utilitarian architecture.

For additional drama, Hans Schmidt (the designing partner) sometimes used color throughout his houses. Unlike Stam, he did not color entire facades but used color to emphasize structural and utilitarian parts. This is especially evident in the Schaeffer House, where the ground floor's walls are white and interior window frames and supporting pillars are black. The ground floor's deliberate sobriety is poor preparation for the carnival feeling of the second floor (plate 2). Assorted pipes and doors that line the main corridor of this floor are painted brilliant primary colors, resulting in imagery reminiscent of Mondrian. This resemblance was not coincidental; Stam, Meyer, and Lissitzky had all been friends of the De Stijl group since the early twenties, and Schmidt was among those who decided to feature works by Mondrian and Vantongerloo in a 1926 issue of *ABC*. It is not surprising then that the sculptural dimensionality of the Colnaghi House bears reminders of Vantongerloo, while Schmidt's interiors reflect the more painterly tendencies of De Stijl. On occasion Schmidt used color externally as well, as in the Huber House in Rhien (1929), where red pilotis form a most unexpected counterpoint to the white house they support (plate 3).

Werner Moser also received several commissions for villas in choice residential areas. The plans for such buildings as the Villa Hagmann (1929–1930) prove that he too was designing floor plans that featured right-angled junctures (figure 4.16). Moser, however, was less fixated on interpenetration; his volumes often only joined at right corners and rarely bisected. His were looser compositions that lacked the centrifugal force inherent in the Artaria and Schmidt versions. Their strength lay in another area.

4.13
Colnaghi House, Basel, 1927–1928, by Paul Artaria and Hans Schmidt. Garden facade. Photo from *ABC*, series 2, no. 4 (1927–1928), p. 9.

4.14
**Colnaghi House, Basel, 1927–
1928, by Paul Artaria and
Hans Schmidt. Garden facade.
Current photo, © 1992 Walter
Mair.**

Moser's houses proved to be outwardly rather than inwardly directed. Frank Lloyd Wright continued to influence his work long after Moser departed Wisconsin; Moser was determined, in particular, that his residential designs should integrate architecture and nature as fluidly as possible. Thus, while his Basel colleagues stressed the knitting of volumes, Moser's houses emphasized a multilevel stepped progression into the surrounding landscape. All of his villas were sited in well-landscaped gardens and photographed when all was in bloom. "Outdoor rooms" and corridors were almost as important to him as indoor areas.

Accordingly, such buildings as Wohnhaus H (1929) and the Villa Hagmann are stepped designs that incorporate expansive terraces on each floor and generous patios at the ground level. At 72 Försterstrasse in Zurich, a villa Moser designed in 1930, terraces descend into the surrounding gardens in stepped formation. To emphasize the effect, terrace partitions repeat this progression (fig-

4.15
Home for Unwed Mothers,
Basel, 1928, by Paul Artaria
and Hans Schmidt. Current
photo, © 1992 Walter Mair.

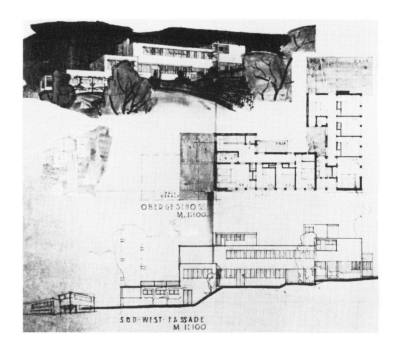

**4.16
Villa Hagmann, Zurich, 1929–
1930, by Werner Moser.
Period drawing.**

ure 4.17). In ABC fashion, industrial-style railings enclosed all out-door spaces, corridors, and external skeletal staircases.

Max Ernst Haefeli and Werner Moser remained close friends throughout the late twenties. Moser shared Haefeli's understanding of interior space while Haefeli admired Moser's embrace of the outdoors. The interior lightness that characterizes the Rotachhäuser is found throughout Moser's interiors as well. They too emphasize light-infused volumes and dramatic staircases that float in generous spaces (figure 4.18).

In 1930, Haefeli received a commission for the first of two exclusive villas in Goldbach, a Zurich suburb. Following earlier ABC examples, Haus K (built in 1931) features bisecting volumes, here presented in T formation. In keeping with Moser's views, the house opens onto natural surroundings. Large windows cover most of the facade, and a network of continuous terraces and outdoor corridors gracefully encircles the rear facade in a manner reminiscent of a small ocean liner. Generous patios lead into a well-landscaped garden. Like Moser's houses, Haus K is clearly a villa for an affluent client who may have been sympathetic to the ABC style but who also valued elegance and comfort. The details and living spaces outside and inside, as in Moser's houses, are well crafted and comfortably laid out. They clearly relate to the needs of the client and the demands of the site.

Artaria and Schmidt were not always as accommodating to clients or to nature. Unlike Moser and Haefeli, Artaria and Schmidt saw their houses as self-involved artistic objects. In 1929 Hans Schmidt and his partner were asked to design a double townhouse in Mexico City (figure 4.19). This commission was probably better suited to Moser's or even Haefeli's talents since the hot climate and exotic locale should have factored into the final design. But Artaria and Schmidt had other ideas. They saw themselves as ABC architects and felt obligated to design a doctrinaire ABC-style house for the site, regardless of its location.

The result was an assemblage of inward-directed volumes lacking expansive terraces or patios that flowed into the landscape. The main outdoor space is a very narrow corridor whose overhead roof and framing pillars define it as an integral part of the enclosed volume. Its purpose seems functional rather than recreational, as it joins the two houses physically and visually. This same lack of enthusiasm for exposure to the elements is evident at the ground level. Each house is relatively closed off from the garden, which can be entered only via a single doorway at the rear of each house; little effort is made to integrate indoors and outdoors beyond that point.

Le Corbusier would certainly have been impressed with the design, and Schmidt would have been most proud of his approval. Le Corbusier was someone Schmidt greatly revered, a figure who may have been partially responsible for the architectural attitude of Schmidt

4.17
72 Försterstrasse, Zurich,
1930, by Werner Moser.
Current photo, © 1992 Walter
Mair.

and Artaria. The following chapters will prove that most of the ABC architects eventually chose instead the constructivist approach that Stam had initiated, one that favored the exposition of structure and function via the use of crystalline walls and structural members that were either externalized or highly visible. Stam had made it very clear in 1925, in the *ABC* article "Modernes Bauen," that Le Corbusier favored an opposite approach based on the manipulation of closed formal volumes and that he did not approve of it.[7]

Schmidt never agreed with Stam on the issue of Le Corbusier, which should not have been surprising in light of Schmidt's background. Unlike the functionally predisposed Stam, Schmidt was educated in the neoclassical tradition of the ETH, the Federal Institute of Technology in Zurich, an institution that stressed the teachings of its great nineteenth-century classical pedagogue, Gottfried Semper. Karl Moser had been trained in Semper's vernacular. Although he later favored a more abstract variant, the senior Moser's work and teachings were rooted in neoclassicism. Hans Schmidt was one of Karl Moser's finest disciples. Although Schmidt did work in Rotterdam and expanded his understanding of radical modernism there, he never could bring himself to reject his neoclassical roots.

Schmidt came to admire Le Corbusier precisely for his manipulation of formal volumes. Prior to 1926 he traveled to Paris to meet him and to study his ideas. It was a most successful meeting. After that trip Schmidt wrote several laudatory essays, including "Le Corbusier als Architekt und Schriftsteller" (Le Corbusier as Architect and Writer) of 1927,[8] and even designed the poster for the exhibition of Le Corbusier's oeuvre in Basel.

In 1928 Schmidt, Stam, and Le Corbusier attended the first Congrès International d'Architecture Moderne (or CIAM) in La Sarraz, Switzerland. At the conference, despite Stam's ongoing hostility toward Le Corbusier, Schmidt and Le Corbusier remained friends. This friendship was fueled by a common acceptance of a classically inspired inclination to create buildings as self-contained entities,

4.18
72 Försterstrasse, Zurich, 1930, by Werner Moser. Interior view of a freestanding stairwell placed in front of a large window. Outdoor "corridor" with industrial railings visible through the window. Current photo, © 1992 Walter Mair.

irrespective of environment. Both believed that buildings should be planar compounds of striking volumetric forms—original sculptural objects and not merely houses.

The Huber House in Rhien, Basel, the most Corbusian of Schmidt's villas, proves this point (figure 4.20; see also plate 3). Here Schmidt did not resort to a Proun-like format. The house is a single rectilinear box raised on ground-level pilotis. The uppermost story is surrounded by a terrace and covered by a thin planar roof. The boundaries of the terrace match those of the roof so that the space can be understood as being within the building, thereby reinforcing the cubic impact of the house. Ultimately, the Huber House is an elegant study in the formal variations on the rectangle, ranging from the small (the windows) to the large (the volume of the house), and from the closed (the side facade, which barely has any windows), to the open (the upper-story terrace). Typical ABC features, such as industrial railings, rarely interfere with this impression. As a result, this building appears far more Corbusian than inspired by ABC constructivism.

These examples illustrate that the private villas of Artaria and Schmidt, Werner Moser, and Max Ernst Haefeli were shaped by sources as diverse as El Lissitzky, Frank Lloyd Wright, and Le Corbusier. Since the above-mentioned houses usually incorporated ABC features they are considered ABC buildings, and exceptionally fine ones at that. However, because of their hybrid sources they cannot be considered ideal representatives of the ABC approach in its purest form.

4.19
Double house, Mexico City, 1929, by Paul Artaria and Hans Schmidt. Garden facade. Archival photo.

4.20
Huber House, Basel, 1929, by
Paul Artaria and Hans Schmidt.
Side view. Archival photo.

Plate 2
Schaeffer House, Basel, 1928,
by Paul Artaria and Hans
Schmidt. Second-story hallway.
Current photo, © 1992 Walter
Mair.

Five

The Glory and Perils of Internationalism

1

Stam, Meyer, and Wittwer: The ABC Masterworks

ABC constructivism finally fulfilled the promise of its early visionary phase—outside of Switzerland. Between 1927 and 1931 Mart Stam, Hans Wittwer, and Hannes Meyer transported the ABC approach to Germany, Holland, and Czechoslovakia. The extraordinary buildings they designed and saw realized in those countries finally proved that ABC constructivism was indeed a viable visionary style.

Since 1924, Mart Stam's oeuvre had continually emphasized Proun-like crystalline volumes in which structure, circulatory parts, and technological elements acted as the main defining features. Regrettably, his low-income housing commissions had not allowed him to demonstrate that unprecedented edifices could be created with this formula. However, after 1926 several private patrons suddenly dis-

5.1
**House in Baba, Prague, 1928–
1932, by Mart Stam. Period
drawing, 1928.**

covered the architect and more ambitious commissions came his
way. These new commissions allowed Stam to fully implement his
approach.

A house Stam designed in 1928 for a housing exhibition in Czechoslovakia illustrates this only too well. As a result of his success at
Weissenhof, Stam was invited by Karel Teige, a leader of the Czech
avant-garde, to design a house for a model housing exhibit in the
Baba district of Prague. The house was finally built between 1930
and 1932 and became a model of Stam's private villa style.

The Czech house was a culmination of all the ideas Stam had
stressed up until this point. It also included one additional feature:
jarring contrasts. Never one to condone predictability, Stam was
determined to prove that he could still shock his audience. To that
end he resorted to a format not seen in his previous work: startling
contrasts between street and rear facades. In the Baba house, the
street facade seems a closely sealed container, with several very
small windows that give the house a hostile and secretive air. The
garden facade is its exact opposite, as an 1928 drawing proves
(figure 5.1). In true ABC fashion, the garden side of the building

metamorphoses into a face of floor-to-ceiling glass, bold structure, interpenetrating Proun-like volumes, outdoor terraces and corridors, and an industrial-style staircase. Additionally, the building conveys a sense of floating lightness since the three-story pillars placed at the front of the facade seem to carry the two upper floors effortlessly. From the garden, the house appears open, radiant, and receptive to people and the elements. While it was common for garden facades to be more open and have larger windows during this period, the extremes of Stam's contrasts between garden and street facades far surpass such expectations. Stam used these contrasts to create a dramatically enriched vision without the use of ornament, symbolism, or expensive materials.

While working on the *ABC* magazine in 1925, Stam accepted a position with the avant-garde architectural firm of Brinkman and Van der Vlugt in Rotterdam. As a result, he spent much of his time in that city and soon became a principal designer in the firm. *ABC* did not suffer from Stam's move; after relocating, he was able to bring a broader international scope to the publication.

In 1928, while working for Brinkman and Van der Vlugt, Stam designed a residence for Kees van der Leeuw, the owner of the Van Nelle company, in Rotterdam.[1] Built between 1928 and 1929, the house attests again to Stam's talent for unexpected contrasts much like those at Baba. From the street this house appears a planar fortresslike structure with insufficient windows, some of which are ominously slitlike (figure 5.2). The rear facade is its opposite, a shimmering study in dematerialization of surfaces and the extremities of structure (plate 4). It is presented as a hierarchical arrangement of virtually transparent volumes. Glass panels of varying dimensions enclose all the interiors. Glass is even used for terrace and roof railings. Once again the architect is not content to design what might easily be a placid facade. He aggressively penetrates these ethereal surfaces with black metal structural frames, similar to those used in his Cornavim project. This violation recalls, on a more subliminal

Kees van der Leeuw House, Rotterdam, 1928–1929, by Mart Stam (for Brinkman and Van der Vlugt). Street facade. Current photo, © 1992 Walter Mair.

level, the sense of astonishment that so many of the early visionary ABC designs were able to evoke.

That same year (1928), Stam designed a house in Ommen, Holland, that was also built. Though small, this dwelling proved to be one of the architect's most developed explorations of the outdoor room concept. Variously framed outdoor spaces create an ongoing dialogue between real interior rooms and the illusory ones that appear around all the levels of the house. Stam's outdoor rooms were further proof that there were successful ways to create an open, "honest" architecture, particularly in a situation in which the budget did not permit the lavish use of glass.

Despite the exemplary nature of Stam's entire oeuvre, one work indisputably stands out as the tour de force of his career: the Van Nelle factory in Rotterdam (figure 5.3 and plate 5). Stam had already begun to plan this extraordinary work as early as 1925 while he

5.3
Van Nelle factory, Rotterdam,
1926–1930, by Mart Stam (for
Brinkman and Van der Vlugt).
Detail of a circulatory tower
housing elevators and stairwells.
Current photo, © 1992 Walter
Mair.

worked for Brinkman and Van der Vlugt. He remained the designer in charge of the project through 1928. Construction on the factory continued through 1930.

While the ABC architects were capable of many fantastic visions, few compare to the scale, intricacy, and impact of this work. The Van Nelle factory is a massive complex of immaculately detailed buildings linked by a huge network of theatrically exposed stairwells, ramps, billboards, and dynamically angled glass bridges. The juxtaposition of these against predominantly glass facades and overt visible structure approximates a futuristic spectacle.

Despite the overwhelming scale that dominates throughout, the details of the project are extremely well controlled and articulated. This is particularly true of the circulatory shafts. These, in the best ABC tradition, are presented as skeletal cages housing elevators and staircases in a variety of configurations—for example, circular stairs and conventional ones juxtaposed for contrast. These types of circulatory shafts act as connecting stations within the larger network of sky-bound bridges that appear everywhere. Their presence further heightens the overall visual activity that occurs at every angle of the factory. With his Rokin and Dam project the architect had promoted the idea that a space-age circulatory system could define, unify, and come to characterize a constructivist complex. In the Van Nelle factory he proved that it could be done.

ABC constructivism inspired two truly outstanding efforts between 1927 and 1931. Stam's Rotterdam factory was the first; Hans Wittwer's Halle Airport restaurant, in Halle, Germany (figures 5.4 and 5.5), was the second.

The Halle Airport restaurant was designed by Wittwer after the dissolution of his partnership with Meyer, which ended over a dispute between 1927 and 1928. According to Wittwer, they had both collaborated on the Federal School of the General German Trade Unions Federation project in Bernau, Germany. Meyer, however

5.4
**Restaurant at Halle Airport,
Halle, Germany,1930—1931,
by Hans Wittwer. Period
photos.**

5.5
**Restaurant at Halle Airport,
Halle, Germany,1930—1931,
by Hans Wittwer. Side view.
Period photo.**

121

publicly claimed complete credit for the work. Indignant, Wittwer left the partnership and set up an independent practice. In 1929 he moved to the city of Halle, Germany, and accepted a teaching position at the School of Arts and Crafts, Burg Giebichenstein. Wittwer's talents were soon brought to the attention of the mayor, Velthuysen. The mayor, a man of enlightened tastes, was so impressed by Wittwer that he helped him secure a part of the commission for the airport that the city was planning to build.

Wittwer was asked to design several buildings for the airport in 1930. The only one that was built was the restaurant building, which was completed the following year. (It was destroyed by bombs in 1940.) The Halle restaurant, an ethereal rectangular box placed behind a forceful staircase-ramp, was the strongest single constructivist statement by an ABC architect to date. The Van Nelle factory was an energetic compound without a single focal point; much of its strength lay in its bold details and component parts. The restaurant was just the opposite. It was a single, overpowering image created solely by two connected components. Wittwer here repeated the approach he and Meyer had devised for the Petersschule project. The Petersschule had consisted of a main building and an enormous ramp that visually had little in common with each other. The former was essentially a human-scaled, closed, rectangular volume, while the latter was an exaggerated, open, triangular form that stressed structural parts.

The Halle Airport restaurant followed this formula in all ways except for one. It is this point of difference that make the Halle restaurant a far more memorable edifice than the Swiss school. At the time the Petersschule was designed, its architects did not yet fully appreciate the powerful imagery that resulted when transparent volumes were contrasted against massive raw structure. By 1930, however, Wittwer had mastered that concept.

The restaurant building embodies the perfect marriage of extremes, with muscular structure consistently played off against small-scale crystalline surfaces. All structural parts, including the staircase ramp and the multistory Y columns that cut through the heart of the restaurant, are aggressively overscaled and opaque. Enveloping the Herculean columns and forming a backdrop to the ramp is a curtain of glass panels that shimmer in daylight or moonlight. This dynamic combination of luminous surfaces, dramatic structure, and extravagant circulatory means yields a breathtaking grandeur unmatched within the ABC movement.

2

Germany: A Utopia Vanishes

The great expectations that seemed so appropriate in 1927, especially in Germany, had eroded by 1929. Unforeseen economic depression brought an end to governmental patronage of modern architecture, and extreme reactionary leaders curtailed ideological tolerance. The era that would bring Hitler, Mussolini, and Stalin to power had begun.

Germany's avant-garde architectural community was devastated by this turn of events. They found themselves increasingly out of favor as the antimodernist rhetoric of such figures as Schultze-Naumburg turned the establishment against radical architects, particularly foreigners and Communists. The three ABC architects who had left Switzerland to reap the benefits of the Weimar Republic's enlightened building programs were immediately affected by these changes.

Mart Stam was not offered any more commissions. After Hellerhof, Stam and May had looked forward to future collaborative efforts in Frankfurt. Unfortunately, the city's Socialist government fell in the wake of Nazism, and with it its progressive building policies. By 1930, it was made clear to May that he was no longer welcome in Frankfurt. May and Stam were thus forced to make other plans.

Hans Wittwer's fate was even sadder. His solo career seemed to be flourishing with the completion of the Halle restaurant. This effort proved that he was eminently capable of noteworthy work in his own right; optimistically he looked forward to more works in Halle and elsewhere. In fact, several potential commissions were on his drawing board after Halle, including one for a Zoological Garden in Basel. But soon Nazism arrived in Halle, and by 1933 the National Socialist Party ruled the city. At the party's insistence, all progressive teachers at the School of Arts and Crafts Burg Giebichenstein were dismissed, including Wittwer.

Wittwer left Halle in 1934, never to return. Disheartened by the turn of events in Halle and the ongoing erosion of modernism, he decided to give up his architectural career forever. After returning to Basel, he entered his family's dairy business and led a very private life until his death in 1952.

While Wittwer's departure from Germany's architectural scene was not a scandalous one, Hannes Meyer's was. Extremely ambitious, Meyer had set his sights on the Bauhaus in 1926. When other ABC architects were joining recognized organizations in order to further their careers, Meyer decided to affiliate himself with the premier avant-garde academy in Europe. He believed that both he and ABC would receive international recognition if the Bauhaus would incorporate their platform. Meyer's quest was initially successful. In 1926, Walter Gropius invited him to establish and head the Bauhaus's architecture faculty. Meyer eagerly accepted and made it clear to Gropius that he intended to emphasize an ABC-oriented program there. In fact on January 18, 1927, he wrote to Gropius that "my teachings will be based on absolutely functional . . . Collectivist . . . Constructive lines in keeping with ABC."[2] Gropius accepted his terms.

True to his word, Meyer instituted a program that stressed functional as well as constructivist values. In order to promote his program, he invited Mart Stam and Hans Wittwer to join the Bauhaus faculty. Stam became a visiting lecturer on elementary building and town planning and Wittwer was designated chief draftsman and lecturer on light, heating, and acoustical installations.

In 1928, Gropius resigned as director and Meyer succeeded him. Once in power Meyer proceeded to redirect the ideological position of the entire school. He developed a curriculum that further stressed the fundamentals of the ABC style and a pro-Marxist position. While numerous faculty members were increasingly uncomfortable with Meyer's extremism, he had reason to feel successful nonetheless. A new generation of Bauhaus students was fascinated by the ideas that he, Stam, and Wittwer were promoting. In fact, several students went on to design ABC-style structures on their own.

As a result of Meyer's powerful position, some important commissions began to come his way. Noteworthy among these was the 1928 commission for the Federal School of the General Trade Unions Federation in Bernau, Germany. This work, which was built between 1928 and 1930, shows a marked departure from the earlier visionary works he had designed with Wittwer. Here, simplicity and restraint prevail over theatricality. Standardization governs the overall design as all functions are relegated to one of two building types: a small residential unit for faculty housing and a larger multistory type for dormitories, classrooms, and assembly rooms.

The plan of this school is truly constructivist. All buildings are dynamically sited in serial zigzag formation within a larger obtuse-angled format. Consequently, there is not a restful space here, as all parts of the complex seem animated. Furthermore, linking the five larger buildings is a prominent corridor, once again showing that circulatory parts were the means that bonded the disparate parts of ABC-style complexes.

The use of zigzag formation as a method of innervation was popularized by Meyer through 1930, as his 1929 competition entry for the ADGB Bank in Berlin proves (figure 5.6). Following ABC precedent, this building is not a singular self-enclosed slab but a long horizontal block flanked by several right-angled wings that alternate between low-rise shed roof structures and high-rise buildings. The latter's jagged contours continue the staccato momentum of the lower shed peaks, as do the zigzag formations within the stair towers. Although the building was never built, it nonetheless proves Meyer's continuing quest to develop the constructivist idiom in unexpected ways.

The buildings of the ABC group and Meyer's own designs in particular were so admired by some of the Bauhaus students that they went on to draft several projects in the ABC style. For example, a single-family residence by Hans Wittwer and his student Hans Volger, designed and built in 1928, recalls aspects of the Swiss villas of Schmidt or Moser. Recalling Schmidt and Artaria's Schaeffer House, it consists of two longitudinal sections that meet on the right angle and are further bound by an outdoor corridor that feeds into a utilitarian metal staircase. Not surprisingly, the upper-story terrace is presented as an outdoor room framed by a cage of poles.

"Project for a School with Eight Classes" (1928) by Ernst Göhl was directly influenced by the German Trade Unions School. Following its example, in the Göhl project functions are separated into repetitive serial pavilions linked by a network of outdoor corridors. This design, however, clearly lacks the novel plan that animated Meyer's complex.

Far more dramatic was the "Project for a School with Thirty-six Classes" by Arieh Sharon and Anton Urban (1929–1930; figure 5.7). Echoing the earlier Meyer-Wittwer Petersschule in plan, this stepped

5.6
ADGB Bank project, Berlin,
1929, by Hannes Meyer.

5.7
"Project for a School with
Thirty-six Classes," Dessau,
Germany, 1929–1930, by
Arieh Sharon and Anton Urban.
Period drawings.

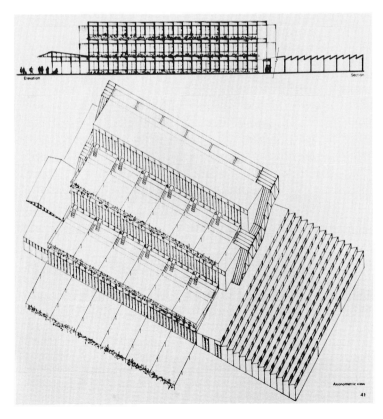

building also calls for a central rectilinear volume flanked by a lower section on one side and a suspended ramp on the other. Here, however, the proportions are reversed. The ramp becomes a minimally scaled overhang over the entry while the classroom wing assumes a far more dominant role. Interesting here is the correspondence between interior and exterior rooms—each classroom has an equivalent outdoor version directly in front of it. Prominent side corridors link the floors in familiar ABC fashion.

Despite his obvious popularity with some of the students, Meyer's tenure as director of the Bauhaus school did not last long or end well. With the rise of Nazism throughout Germany, it was increasingly clear that Jews, leftists, Communists, and foreigners were no longer welcome. Germany's extravagant honeymoon with the international avant-garde and with Meyer was over. On July 29, 1930, he was openly accused of being a Marxist by the mayor of Dessau and fired from his post.

By 1930, ABC could no longer be the international movement it had been. With widespread economic depression affecting Europe, there were few commissions available anywhere, particularly for radicals. Stam, Meyer, and Wittwer recognized that they could not continue to work in Holland and Germany.

Only one European nation was an exception to this trend: Switzerland. Politically neutral and economically stable, it continued to offer opportunities for its architects. Thus, while Meyer, Stam, and Wittwer found themselves unemployed, the same was not true for those ABC architects who had remained in Switzerland.

But these three men were not willing to return to Switzerland as architects. They still regarded Switzerland as a backwater within Europe's architectural community. In three brief years they had designed some of Europe's outstanding buildings and had come to rule its most prestigious school of architecture. Returning to Switzerland would mean that they had given up on their dream of creating an international constructivist movement in which they were the rising stars. Furthermore, they were not prepared to settle in a country that was inhospitable to Communists. Wittwer remained in Halle until his retirement in 1934, but Meyer and Stam were ready for new horizons.

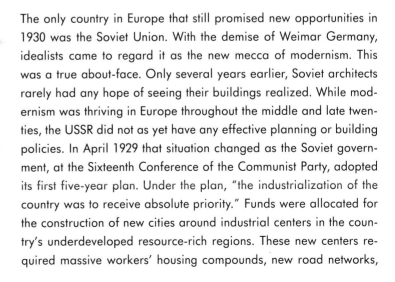

3

The USSR: A Promise Unfulfilled

The only country in Europe that still promised new opportunities in 1930 was the Soviet Union. With the demise of Weimar Germany, idealists came to regard it as the new mecca of modernism. This was a true about-face. Only several years earlier, Soviet architects rarely had any hope of seeing their buildings realized. While modernism was thriving in Europe throughout the middle and late twenties, the USSR did not as yet have any effective planning or building policies. In April 1929 that situation changed as the Soviet government, at the Sixteenth Conference of the Communist Party, adopted its first five-year plan. Under the plan, "the industrialization of the country was to receive absolute priority." Funds were allocated for the construction of new cities around industrial centers in the country's underdeveloped resource-rich regions. These new centers required massive workers' housing compounds, new road networks, and assorted communal facilities. By 1930, such construction was under way, proving that expansive opportunities now existed in that country.

Soviet architects, largely inexperienced at this point, were overwhelmed by the new tasks given them. Recognizing this problem, the Soviet government invited foreign architects and planners to come and supervise the large-scale undertakings. These were precisely the opportunities Meyer and Stam were looking for in 1930. They believed that they had not yet reached the pinnacle of their careers and that the Soviet Union now afforded them the opportunity to do so.

Their willingness to go there was not as opportunistic as it may seem. Though ABC had rejected the impractical Asnova approach in 1927, Stam and Meyer had never rejected the USSR, Communism, or any serious commitment to building. Once the USSR changed its official policies, these men were only too eager to affiliate themselves with a country that was seeking to develop itself along practical lines.

Two months after his dismissal from the Bauhaus, Meyer convinced six Bauhaus students to emigrate to the USSR with him. They came to be known as the Bauhaus Brigade. Extremely optimistic about his relocation, Meyer stated prior to departing Germany:

After many years of working in the capitalist system I am convinced that working under such conditions is quite senseless. In view of our Marxist and revolutionary conception of the world we, the revolutionary architects, are at the mercy of the insoluble contradictions of the world built on animal individualism and the exploitation of man by man. I have said and I say again, to all architects, all engineers, all builders: "Our way is and must be that of the revolutionary proletariat, that of the communist party, the way of those who are building and achieving socialism."

*I am leaving for the U.S.S.R. to work among people who are
forging a true revolutionary culture, who are achieving socialism, and who are living in that form of society for which we
have been fighting here under the conditions of capitalism.*

*I beg our Russian comrades to regard us, my group and myself,
not as heartless specialists claiming all kinds of special privi-
leges, but as fellow workers with comradely views ready to make
a gift to socialism and the revolution of all our knowledge, all
our strength, and all our experience that we have acquired in
the art of building.*[3]

Stam and Ernst May also accepted the Soviet offer. May and Stam chose to go together and brought with them over twenty members of the team that had worked on the mass housing projects in Frankfurt.

Joining May and Stam was Hans Schmidt. The most talented and radical of the Swiss ABC members, he too was ready to leave his own country. Believing that he had fulfilled his potential in Switzerland, he saw his future alongside Stam and Meyer. In 1931 he wrote: "The USSR affords us not merely opportunities in the area of architecture. . . . It also affords us the opportunity to partake in the initial realization of the classless society of workers. Architecture is the means toward this end."[4] In the fall of 1930 he terminated his partnership with Artaria and departed.

Meyer and Schmidt had great hopes for success in the USSR. Despite their claims to the contrary, these men had grown accustomed to recognition and positions of authority and expected to find more of the same there. They were convinced that they could make a difference and would contribute in the area of town planning—an area on which Europe had not concentrated seriously enough.

Town planning had always been one of the fundamental tenets of the ABC position. ABC's founders saw buildings as part of larger town planning schemes. In fact, *ABC* magazine's inaugural issue featured several significant articles on town planning. ABC's ideas on the subject were highly influenced by the writings of Friedrich Engels, particularly *Zur Wohnungsfrage* (1887), which served as a guideline for the housing policies established in postrevolutionary Russia. Engels's treatise emphasized that economic crises and the problems created by class-ridden societies would end once land and manufacturing concessions were removed from private ownership. A socialized state with new cities was a part of the correct solution. The new cities were to be sited around production centers that provided employment and housing to all citizens. Such housing was to be nonhierarchical and would thereby pave the way for a long-awaited egalitarian society. Engels's views influenced postrevolutionary Russia's plans, which called for cities with specific production zones and massive workers' housing complexes in adjacent zones.

In 1923, Mart Stam had drafted an outline in which he described his version of such a city. Stam's version additionally emphasized access to the nonurban countryside via a road network that led out of the city into open green vistas. He brought his reverence of the natural landscape into his plans for inner cities as well by stressing green zones that included parks and recreational areas. This emphasis on natural surroundings was a Dutch concept that such architects as Granpre Moliere, Stam's Rotterdam employer and mentor, articulated in their own planning schemes.

Between 1923 and 1928 Stam developed plans that underscored all of these interests. The *Schweizerische Bauzeitung* published one of the earliest in 1923. Stam stated:

The truly modern city is a composite of necessary functions and requirements. Clearly demarcated spaces must be established for all its concerns, and these include residential sections, industrial quarters, commercial centers, recreational areas, and parks.

Properly defined spaces must be designed for roads, avenues, railroad terminals, and tram lines. . . .

The city of the Middle Ages was a closed city, surrounded by a wall. . . . The new city is open. . . . It is concerned about the health of its residents. Therefore all efforts are made to extend and merge the city grid with outlying regions.[5]

Stam called for better town planning solutions and *ABC* decided to provide them. Schmidt and Stam went on to develop schemes, based on Stam's earlier guideline, that were intended for contemporary industrial cities and recognized both the needs of the working class and those of the developing state. Separate sections were designated for residential, recreational, commercial, and industrial use. While conditions of terrain determined where these zones would be located, a network of roads based on functional rather that formal considerations would link the sections and extend into the countryside.

In "Das Chaos im Stadtbau," which appeared in the first issue of the magazine, Hans Schmidt proposed precisely such a redevelopment plan for his native Basel. According to Schmidt, his scheme was completely functional, based solely on considerations of need and topography, following no preconceived formal plan. Basel was to be divided into sectors for housing and industry, with a large nature belt and hospital forming the boundary between them. The siting of each zone was determined by wind patterns and land conditions. Adequate circulation would be provided by streets laid out to best meet each zone's specific needs. The industrial zone would connect to a highway network while the streets of the residential area would radiate into the scenic countryside.[6]

Later *ABC* issues reinforced these points. In 1926 appeared Mart Stam's proposal for the city of Trautenau, Czechoslovakia.[7] It emphasized the same requisites as the Basel plan. Stam argued for decentralized traffic plans that were based on function and not on an a priori beaux-arts plan.

While ABC architects had succeeded in building ABC-style buildings in Europe, they had not as yet had any opportunities to realize their ultimate goal, that of planning an ideal ABC city. Meyer, Stam, and Schmidt believed that the Soviet Union now afforded them this opportunity on a grand scale. But they were soon to be disappointed.

Initially Meyer, Stam, and Schmidt had little grasp of the realities they would encounter in the USSR. The glorious commissions they expected to find there did not exist for foreigners. Instead of authorities eager to allow them to build buildings or cities, they found a disorganized bureaucracy too confused to declare winners in competitions and official policies that prevented any foreign architect from designing an entire large-scale project. Both factors resulted in collaborative team efforts; the Soviet Union did not prove to be their locale for individual glory.

Hannes Meyer's experience with the Moscow Town Soviet exemplifies what these men encountered in the USSR. After Meyer first arrived in Moscow, he accepted a professorship at the Vasi School of Architecture in Moscow within the Department of Housing and Social Engineering. He assumed that shortly thereafter he would receive building assignments in Moscow, but this did not prove to be the case. In 1931, the Moscow Town Soviet elected to redevelop the city of Moscow; instead of giving the task to one architect or group of architects, it chose a far more complicated approach. For each Moscow site, eight collaborative submissions were required. Each submission was designed by a "brigade" that consisted of one architect in charge of a small consortium of planners and architects. Meyer was asked, along with his Bauhaus Brigade, to be one of the eight entrants. His group, which included Arieh Sharon, Konrad Püschel, and Tibor Weiner, prepared numerous plans for the Moscow scheme. They were submitted, along with those of the seven other brigades. Much to the frustration of all the entrants, the range of submissions proved too confusing to the judging Town Soviet leaders and none could be agreed upon.

The years between 1931 and 1934 were not productive ones for Meyer, at least not in the manner he had originally anticipated. He continued to teach at the Vasi School through 1933, moving from one faculty to another. In addition to the above-cited departments, he also taught in those of agriculture and industrial building. With his Bauhaus Brigade he worked on schemes for the town of Kerch, a technical college and factory in Giprovtus, and a school in Gorki. Meyer often acted as overseer while his former students designed the individual buildings. He was also designated chief architect within departments that planned such centers of heavy industry as Molotov and Nizhniy Kurinsk and the cities of Birobidjan, Krasnoyarsk, and Rybinsk. Although cities such as Sozgorod Gorki (1932) were built or partially built, as was Nizhniy Kurinsk (1932), they were for the most part collaborative efforts that resulted in barracks-type housing and spartan larger buildings. The monuments to constructivism that Meyer had envisioned were not economically feasible or desirable in such remote and cold areas.[8] Furthermore, Stalin did not prove to be an advocate of constructivism, favoring a reactionary neoclassicism instead.

The fate that befell Stam, May, and Schmidt was similar to Meyer's. They too had come directly to Moscow in the fall of 1930 to join the Standardgorproyet, the bureau established by Soviet authorities to delegate building and planning assignments to the newly arriving foreign architects. The three men, along with May's Frankfurt disciples, who included Fred Forbat, formed their own brigade. Among the group, Stam had the most luck. His brigade won the competition for the city of Magnitogorsk in Siberia. Placed in charge of the project, Stam actually lived on the construction site for three years overseeing the construction of bland, indistinguishable low-rise housing sections. Stam was able to design and supervise only one district within a city planned for 200,000, since the Moscow authorities insisted that other architects be given the same opportunities as this foreigner.

In 1932, Stam was transferred to a new project: the development of the much smaller town of Makeyevka. For the next year he worked on the plans for this city of 17,000 inhabitants. As he had done in Magnitogorsk, he devised an overall city plan that segmented the municipality into separate zones for separate functions, in accordance with the contours of the difficult terrain. Emphasis was placed, in true ABC fashion, on an open traffic plan that best suited the area and radiated into the outlying landscape. Only part of Stam's plan was adopted, and was later executed by Czech architects.[9]

If Stam believed that his limited successes would lead to larger and more complete assignments, he, like Meyer, was destined for disappointment. His next master plan was for the city of Orsk in 1934. Once again he developed a decentralized ABC-style scheme. This time, however, it was not well received. The Russians in charge decided on a more centralized format and rejected Stam's work. Rather than revise his original plan, Stam left the job and asked Hans Schmidt to take charge in his stead. Stam was then asked to plan Balgash. After studying the site, he informed the authorities that the terrain was too difficult for construction. Stam's opinion was once again not well received. He soon found himself out of favor with the Soviet authorities.

Increasing criticism of Stam had little to do with his talents. The spirit of hospitality that had opened the doors of the Soviet Union to sympathetic foreigners had disappeared by 1934. As Stalin's power increased, his tolerance of outsiders, especially modernist architects, decreased. The USSR, entering a reactionary era marked by acute nationalism and strict economic self-preservation, was increasingly unwilling to grant available work to non-Soviets. It soon became clear to Stam and May that they were no longer welcome there, and in 1934 they departed. Meyer left two years later.

Hans Schmidt remained in the USSR until 1937. According to manuscripts he wrote between 1931 and 1937, he had arrived with largely ideological aspirations. He had come to see whether ABC ideology could be adapted there. By 1933, in an essay entitled "Was ist richtig?," he admitted that the talents of the Western architects were not being fulfilled in the USSR,[10] but his commitment to Communism was so strong that he stayed despite the changing political climate. In 1937 he finally concluded that his original optimism was unfounded. In the article "Die sowjetische Architektur und das Problem des Monumentalen" (1937) he expressed his regret that the nation that had given rise to Asnova and constructivism was now regressing to Stalin's much preferred neoclassicism.[11]

The years in the Soviet Union proved to be more than a disappointing experience for Stam, Meyer, and Schmidt. They had arrived as rising international stars and within a few years were reduced to the level of collaborators, with relatively little work or accolades to show for the time spent there. Furthermore, Stalin's policies destroyed the architects' Marxist hopes for a new society. They left emotionally broken men who would never again gather the enthusiasm that they had exhibited in their ABC years.

Unsure of their destinations upon departing, Stam and Schmidt opted for the obvious solution; they returned to their home cities. Stam came back to Rotterdam in 1934. Due to the darkening economic and political conditions, it was hard for him to find work. Early in 1936 he was able to design and build a row of flats on the Anthony van Dijckstraat. Designed in collaboration with van Tijen and his wife, Lotte Stam Beese, the flats proved that the spirit of ABC still lingered. These were simple three-story flats with terraces on the garden facades and ribbon windows facing the street. They incorporated one obvious ABC feature: entry was not from the street level but from the second floor, via an open ladder-type staircase. Unfortunately, these flats were among the last of Stam's designs to be built for at least twenty years.

Stam continued to design for a while longer. In 1937, again with Lotte Stam Beese and van Tijen, he submitted an entry for the design competition for the Town Hall of Amsterdam. By now it was clear that the architect was drained of his innovative zest. Although the complex offered a right-angled constructivist plan and much glass, it was hardly a design that could inspire much enthusiasm—certainly not when compared to the winning entry by Berghoef and Vegter, a far more flamboyant design that proved how staid Stam had become in comparison. By the end of the decade, Stam's career as one of the century's ideological and stylistic trailblazers was over.

Over the following years Stam developed a reclusive personality. During the forties he entered several competitions and in the late fifties and early sixties he did see some of his apartment building designs realized in Amsterdam. Increasingly secretive, he retired to Switzerland in 1966, refusing to see anyone from the architectural community. He died there in 1986.

Hans Schmidt suffered a similar fate in Basel. Both his former partner and the Swiss establishment had lost interest in him. After Schmidt's move to the USSR, Artaria's career continued to flourish. Commissions for villas in the Basel area that would normally have gone to the partners now went to Artaria alone. Artaria was so proud of his solo achievements that he published the book *Vom Bauen und Wohnen* (1948), which catalogued his post-1930 oeuvre.[12] Successful and content on his own, he had no reason to rejoin the partner who had overshadowed and finally abandoned him. As for the Swiss establishment, it was less than eager to give any commissions to a man who had so conspicuously left their country in favor of the Soviet Union and Communism.

The only commission Schmidt did receive was for a contagious diseases wing for the Basler Burgspital, which was not completed until 1945. A sleek and elegant building, it had little to say that was original. Increasingly disheartened by his inability to find suitable work and uncomfortable in so staid a society, Schmidt migrated to East Germany in 1956. He remained there, teaching architecture and planning, and did not return to Basel until 1970, two years before his death.

Equally demoralized by the years in the Soviet Union, Meyer was also unable to reestablish himself after departing in 1936. He went briefly to Czechoslovakia and then returned to Switzerland in 1937, finding limited opportunities available to him. Still adventurous by nature, he finally chose to migrate to Mexico, where he believed there was a future for a Marxist like himself. In 1939, he agreed to become the director of the Instituto de Urbanismo y Planificación in Mexico City. Through the coming years he also assumed teaching positions and held highly respected positions on the municipal planning commission.

But his era as a constructivist architect was over. Town planning was his main occupation in Mexico. His new profession could not have been altogether satisfying; several drawings for a development in Manzana de Corpus Christi, Mexico, of 1947 prove that constructivism was still very much on his mind. These were grand elaborations that recalled his heroic visions of the twenties. He died in 1954 without seeing any of them realized.

Plate 6
Freibad Allenmoos, Zurich, 1938–1939, by Werner Moser and Max Ernst Haefeli. The intersection of the restaurant and game room sections. Current photo, © 1992 Walter Mair.

CIAM, *Weiterbauen*, and the Perpetuation of the ABC Legacy in Switzerland

1

ABC and CIAM

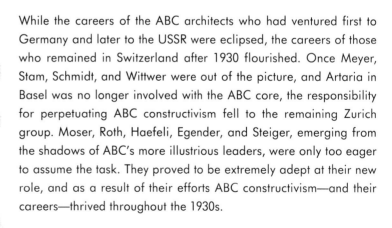

While the careers of the ABC architects who had ventured first to Germany and later to the USSR were eclipsed, the careers of those who remained in Switzerland after 1930 flourished. Once Meyer, Stam, Schmidt, and Wittwer were out of the picture, and Artaria in Basel was no longer involved with the ABC core, the responsibility for perpetuating ABC constructivism fell to the remaining Zurich group. Moser, Roth, Haefeli, Egender, and Steiger, emerging from the shadows of ABC's more illustrious leaders, were only too eager to assume the task. They proved to be extremely adept at their new role, and as a result of their efforts ABC constructivism—and their careers—thrived throughout the 1930s.

The Zurich group had the assistance of a larger established organization, the Congrès Internationaux d'Architecture Moderne (CIAM). In 1928, the year of *ABC Beiträge zum Bauen*'s demise, CIAM was founded in La Sarraz, Switzerland. It was intended as an impartial collective of architects who sought to promote the international development of modern architecture and planning. ABC's members soon learned to manipulate the organization to gain recognition of the ABC position and to help establish a vehicle by which the ABC legacy could continue to evolve through the 1930s.

CIAM's large membership was international and not representative of any single position. The notables who made up its ranks included H. P. Berlage, Pierre Chareau, Josef Frank, Gabriel Guevrékian, Hugo Häring, Huib Hoste, Le Corbusier, Pierre Jeanneret, André Lurçat, Fernando Garcia Mercadal, Carlo Rava, Gerrit Rietveld, Alberto Sartoris, H. Von der Mühll, and Karl Moser. These architects, many of whom were already well known, spoke for a modernist constituency that often sympathized with leftist causes but was itself not necessarily affiliated with a Communist or Marxist network. Despite the fact that they represented a more extreme point of view, Hannes Meyer, Hans Schmidt, Paul Artaria, Mart Stam, Werner Moser, Rudolf Steiger, Max Ernst Haefeli, and Stam's friend Ernst May also joined.

The members of CIAM resolved to draft a charter delineating the position of the organization with regard to building and planning during the inaugural year. They also elected Karl Moser president. It was Moser's duty to organize those meetings in which the contents of the official CIAM charter were to be determined. As might be expected from so diverse a membership, numerous proposals were announced at these meetings, ranging from the inclusion of Le Corbusier's Five Points to an adoption of a far more more radical ABC-inspired position.

It was Hans Schmidt, acting as the ABC spokesperson, who insisted on a socially relevant ABC-oriented platform. Although the ABC members were among the least-known participants at the conference, they were nonetheless determined to steer the CIAM charter in their direction. The group's confidence was not unwarranted since they did have one distinct advantage—Karl Moser's loyalty.

ABC's members correctly assumed that CIAM President Karl Moser would be supportive of his son's and his former students' demands. Accordingly, the group came up with a plan that was predicated on his cooperation. Moser was informed of the group's plan of action long before it was enacted. As early as April 27, 1928, two months before the conference, Schmidt wrote a letter to Moser that pointedly stated that he and and his fellow Dutch and Swiss architects advocated a radical "propaganda"-oriented position. Later, at the conference, the so-called "Swiss and Dutch architects" openly insisted that Schmidt's ideological program be adopted by the entire CIAM assembly. They threatened to withdraw their active support of the organization and serve only as "guests" if Schmidt's position was not favored over those of a more establishment-oriented nature.[1]

The ABC campaign succeeded, not because of its militancy but because of Karl Moser's bias. The ensuing "La Sarraz Declaration" reflected ABC's ideas. The document asserted that architecture was not a function of style or the social dictates of the reigning establishment, but rather the product of technical innovation, standardization, and production. In addition, it advocated functional town planning and new social policies intended to benefit all members of society.

ABC sustained its strength within CIAM even after La Sarraz. With Karl Moser's ongoing support, the group continued to campaign for the implementation of town planning and low-cost working-class housing. At the second conference, "Die Wohnung für das Existenzminimum," which was held in Frankfurt in 1929, ABC's outspokenness was rewarded once again. Stam and Schmidt were recognized as authorities on the above subjects and assumed new prominence within the organization. The next year, at the 1930 "Rationelle Bebauungsweisen" meeting in Brussels, the impact of ABC was obvious. The virtues of low-cost, low-maintenance, standardized housing were lauded, and the Schorenmatten, WOBA Eglisee, and Neubühl developments were cited as outstanding examples of this kind of housing.

After the first two conferences it was clear that ABC owed its growing popularity to the charismatic personalities of Stam, Meyer, and Schmidt. They had come to be regarded as avant-garde leaders whose work and ideas were of interest to everyone there. Eager to maintain their status at the third conference, the three prepared a surprise for their CIAM audience. In Brussels, Stam, Meyer, and Schmidt announced that they were leaving for Russia immediately after the close of the conference.

Their revelation created a sensation. Suddenly these three were seen as heroic pioneers, and the attention of CIAM focused on their brave ambition. The conferees cheered their gesture, and in honor of "Brigade May" (which included May, Stam, and Schmidt) and Brigade Meyer (a group of former Bauhaus students led by Meyer), CIAM decided to hold its next conference in Moscow.

The Moscow meeting never materialized. Discussions with the Russians regarding the upcoming conference were as unsuccessful as the careers of the Europeans who had gone there to work. After three years of endless delays and breakdowns in negotiations, CIAM finally gave up on the Moscow plan and decided to hold its fourth meeting in Athens instead.

The loss of interest in the Russian conference paralleled CIAM's decreasing interest in Stam, Schmidt, Meyer, and May. By 1933 it had become clear that these architects' grand expectations were not being realized. Although such works as the Orsk plans were shown at the fourth conference, it was fairly obvious that these men did not have anything exceptional to show for their years in Russia. By the time of the fourth CIAM conference, they were relatively forgotten. The remaining ABC members, however, were not.

The fourth CIAM conference, "Die funktionelle Stadt," was held in three parts. The first part of the conference took place on July 29, 1933, aboard the ship *Patris II.* The second part convened in Athens on August 3, and the final part occurred eight days later as the participants were homeward bound on the *Patris II.* Among the conference's notable developments was the emergence of the Zurich-based ABC faction as the carrier of the ABC banner. Emil Roth, Werner Moser, Haefeli, Steiger, and two relatives, Hans Schmidt's brother Georg and Emil's younger second cousin Alfred Roth, took control of the Swiss contingent and assumed prominence within CIAM. It was the Zurich group's intention to actively promote ABC. They remembered the lesson of 1927, namely, that affiliation with a recognized organization was the best route toward larger recognition. Since CIAM was the source of such support at the time, they resolved to function as a CIAM subgroup.

Together with Alfred Roth and Georg Schmidt, the Zurich group conceived a plan of action. Recalling how well *ABC Beiträge zum Bauen* had advanced ABC's causes in the early years, they decided once again to issue a periodical inspired by ABC's ideals. Approaching the CIAM members aboard the *Patris II,* they offered to issue a small magazine reviewing CIAM-related issues in architecture and planning if the organization would provide the funds. Their proposal was accepted.

2

Weiterbauen, 1934–1936

The ABC members named the new magazine *Weiterbauen,* a title that expressed their intention to continue to build (figure 6.1). The first issue of *Weiterbauen,* which came to be recognized as the official magazine of the "Schweizergruppe" (Swiss group) of CIAM, appeared in September 1934. Five more issues were published before its demise in December 1936. Despite its short life span, *Weiterbauen*'s impact was profound. The new publication proved that ABC was still a significant movement despite the departure of Stam, Wittwer, Schmidt, and Meyer. Gone, however, was the radical spirit and international point of view that had been a part of the movement's essence through 1930.

november 1934 jahrgang 1 heft **2** zusammengestellt durch die schweizergruppe der INTERNATIONALEN KONGRESSE FÜR NEUES BAUEN

erscheint jährlich sechs mal als beiblatt der schweizer bauzeitung und in oeren verlag, zürich. dianastrasse 5. telephon 34507. postscheck VIII 6110.

für abonnenten der schweizer bauzeitung gratis „weiterbauen" allein 5 fr. ausland 6 fr. einzelheft 1 fr.

DISKUSSIONSBLATT FÜR DIE PROBLEME DES NEUEN BAUENS UND VERWANDTER GEBIETE

6.1

Opening page of *Weiterbauen*, 2 (November 1934).

In theory, *Weiterbauen* was established to document those CIAM activities that were of interest to the Swiss CIAM faction. Ultimately, however, its greatest contribution was its chronicling of the evolution of ABC constructivism between 1930 and 1936. The magazine proved that despite ideological shifts, ABC constructivism was a viable style capable of flourishing in unexpected directions. ABC constructivism of the thirties had grown into a rich mannerist variant of the original style, placing emphasis on shocking contrasts, animation, diffraction, monumentality, and finally on the dematerialization and structural primacy that Stam had insisted on. Until this time, the Swiss ABC architects had not been ready to fully adopt Stam's methods, and it is ironic that they chose to do so only after his departure.

Weiterbauen was founded by CIAM's then president, Dr. Sigfried Giedion (another Swiss national), Alfred Roth, Werner Moser, Rudolf Steiger, and Ernst F. Burckhardt. Giedion's position was only honorary, leaving actual control in the hands of the pro-ABC faction and Burckhardt, Egender's new partner. Egender had officially joined CIAM in 1932, at the time that he and Burckhardt had joined forces.

Weiterbauen was an imitation of *ABC Beiträge zum Bauen*, but a very weak one. Without Lissitzky's, Stam's, and Schmidt's design talents, *Weiterbauen* qualified even less as a work of art than had the *ABC* magazine, since its pages were essentially diluted imitations of the latter. Its more reserved and conventional format was in keeping with its more moderate ideological perspective.

The first two issues, both in 1934, focused on the fourth CIAM conference. In addition to reviews of the conference, they featured richly illustrated essays that detailed the past and current state of town planning in Europe and discussed New York as well. Recalling *ABC*'s ecumenical approach, there were also articles on building, such as an essay by Alfred Roth on roof types.[2] Issue 2 promoted planning-related issues and discussed the work of Hans Arp, Alberto Giacometti, and Le Corbusier. Following ABC precedent, the magazine also paid homage to other small international publications. Brief synopses of articles from *Opbouw* (Holland), *Quadrante* (Italy), and the *Architectural Record* (USA) appeared on the last page of the issue.

Issues 3 and 4, of 1935, were very similar to those of the previous year. Both discussed the arts as well as building. CIAM conferences could not be discussed, simply because there weren't any; the next conference was not held until 1937. Instead, both issues focused on Zurich's Kunstgewerbemuseum (still the domain of Alfred Altherr of the Swiss Werkbund) and its exhibition on the bath and the bathhouse entitled "Das Bad von heute und gestern" (The Bath: Today and Yesterday).

In issue 5 of January 1936, a long overdue overview of architectural projects and built commissions by CIAM's Swiss group finally appeared. The examples shown in this issue were by the remaining ABC group, Alfred Roth, and their colleagues. Although not all the buildings featured in issue 5 represented the ABC viewpoint, the issue nonetheless contained the most comprehensive overview of post-1930 ABC constructivism available at that time. Its contents startled those who had assumed that ABC's relevance was over. Abundant with designs, most of which were built, issue 5 vividly proved that the ABC approach had been successfully redefined to suit the 1930s.

Issue 5 illustrated in proposal form Werner Moser's Student Union Building for the University of Basel (1932), Burckhardt's Basel Canton Bank, an apartment block by Egender and Wilhelm Müller (1933), a single-family home by Haefeli, and a school in Altstetten by Alfred Roth (1932). Shown in photographic form in their built state were the Doldertal houses by Alfred and Emil Roth, with Marcel Breuer, Egender, and Burckhardt's Johanniskirche in Basel, Steiger's General Motors factory in Biel, Emil Roth's Deuchler House, as well as Egender and Müller's Alfred House. In order to prove that modernism was coming into its own in their country, the editors also included buildings by other avant-garde architects that echoed ABC's approach in their reductive simplicity. Selected were Senn and Mock's Parkhaus Zossen in Basel, Alfred Altherr's Landhaus in Herrliberg, the Lagerhaus in Köniz by H. Brechbühler, Kellermüller and Hofmann's Wohn-Kolonie Oeristeig, and the most traditional structure in the group, H. Fischli's abstract version of a chalet in Herrliberg.

After 1930 architectural taste in general evolved in a mannerist direction. Many of the above designs and those discussed in the next section illustrate how, and ultimately why, the remaining ABC group also adopted a mannerist approach. Among the first buildings that reflected this shift was the Kunstgewerbeschule and Museum in Zurich by Egender and Steger (1930–1932), cited in issue 4.

Until this time, most ABC works in Switzerland were of a low-rise, residential nature, especially Egender and Steger's. Egender had designed such dynamic low-rise structures as the Kusnacht bathing club restaurant (1928–1930) and Zurich's Zoological Garden restaurant (1929), which too was vivid in its structural articulation and strong forms. He also designed homes on Wunderliststrasse and Schwendenhausstrasse (1929) in Zurich. Both of these homes recalled the spartan housing that Stam had introduced at Weissenhof in 1927: crisp, barren rectangles distinguished only by industrial railings, exposed porches, roof terraces, and exterior staircases.

In many respects the Kunstgewerbeschule and Museum reflects earlier ABC work. It consists of three undecorated rectangular sections connected at right angles. In an effort to express that each section houses separate functions, each differs in height, size, and fenestration pattern. Visual emphasis is also granted to stairwells. What is new, however, is the explosion in scale. Until this time ABC's members had designed large edifices mainly for foreign cities; the Zurich school and museum was among the first monumental ABC-style public buildings to be built in Switzerland.

Also unexpected at Egender and Steger's complex are the staggering contrasts between mass and volume. By 1930 one had come to expect shocking contrasts from Stam and Wittwer, but not from architects like Egender and Steger who had remained in Zurich. At the Kunstgewerbeschule and Museum, not only do such contrasts appear throughout but they take a new form. The dialogue here is not between structure and surface but between the exterior and the interior, as the massive exteriors give way to a surprising diffusion of walls inside the buildings. Walls often disappear, and as a result ABC-style stairwells float within expanses of glass while hallways and classrooms maintain a sense of openness. This is particularly evident along those luminous corridors where the upper dividing walls between classrooms, and between hallways and classrooms, are made of glass panels (figure 6.2). Whereas Haefeli's Rotachhäuser had anticipated such interiors on a limited scale (see figure 4.6), these interiors now enter the mainstream of post-1930 ABC constructivism.

6.2
Kunstgewerbeschule and Museum, Zurich, 1930–1931, by Karl Egender and Adolf Steger. View of glass-paneled partitions between classrooms. Current photo, © 1992 Walter Mair.

**Student Union Building of the
University of Basel, project,
1932, by Werner Moser, as
shown in *Weiterbauen*, 5
(January 1936), p. 3.**

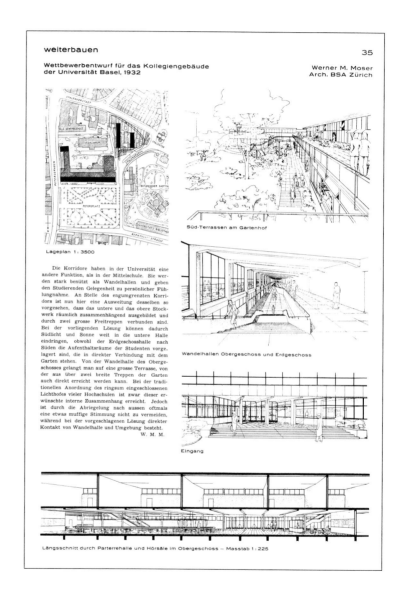

Werner Moser's 1932 proposal for the Student Union Building of the University of Basel (figure 6.3) further elaborates many of the same ideas. The scheme resorts to a constructivist-inspired plan that relies on joined right angles; the main building is a familiar compound of pavilions that are encircled by outdoor corridors, ramps, and prominent staircases. As usual, Moser has these descend in stepped progression into the gardens, which play a notable role in the overall plan. New here for Moser is the large scale of the work as well as its transparency. Following Stam's example, predominantly glass walls elucidate interior functions and the structural system, which in this case is Stam's preferred portal frame system. Not only does Moser use the portal frame throughout the interior, he extends the frames to the open areas of the ground level as well, years after Stam's Cornavim. The student union project is unquestionably larger, more structurally relevant, and more dematerialized than any edifice Moser had designed in Switzerland. While it is true that the crystalline Pearcon Street project (see figure 3.10) had been grander, that was a fantasy project drawn in the United States for a Chicago site that required a skyscraper. On his return to Switzerland, Moser had initially adopted the more small-scaled, low-rise format discussed earlier. In the student union project he merged his nature-oriented villa style with Pearcon Street's expansiveness and emphasis on structure.

Residential designs by the ABC architects during this period also reflect the changes in their approach. Emil Roth's house for Dr. Deuchler in Zurich, built in 1934, stands out among these (figure 6.4). At first glance the house looks like an archetypal ABC building of the twenties (in fact few buildings, even by ABC, were ever this spartan). It appears to be a pristine white box with an austere arrangement of windows and an undistinguished entrance. To enhance the sense of austerity, an inelegant chain link fence encircles the roof. Fully examining the roof level, however, one finds something startlingly different (figure 6.5). Within the fence-enclosed space sits an exquisite glass box that is the antithesis of all the staid and rectilinear elements of the house. Multifaceted and crystalline, it is

6.4
Dr. Deuchler House, Zurich, 1934 by Emil Roth. Period photo.

further vivified by a dramatically cantilevered roof that recalls the thrust of the one Egender had designed for the Kusnacht bath club. It is precisely this unexpected juxtaposition of the rigid and utilitarian against the dramatic and elegant that places the house in the post-twenties era in which multivalent imagery came to typify ABC designs.

Reflecting this multivalency in an altogether different manner are two houses that Alfred and Emil Roth designed with Marcel Breuer and built in the Doldertal section of Zurich in 1935 (figure 6.6). Breuer's union with the Roths was not out of character, as his career had entered a quasi-constructivist phase at this time.[3] Breuer received his first architectural commission from a wealthy German industrialist named Harnischmacher, for a villa in Wiesbaden, Germany. Although one cannot prove that the Harnischmacher House (1932) was ABC-inspired, Breuer did separate the house into distinct functional sections, and did change roof levels to distinguish each section. He also designed a street facade that is almost windowless

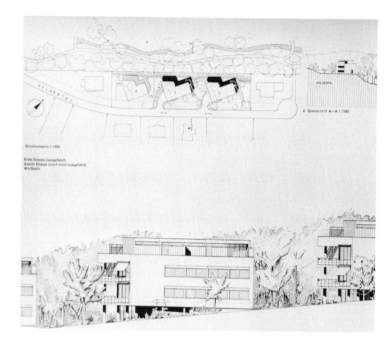

6.6
Doldertal houses, Zurich, 1935, by Alfred Roth, Emil Roth, and Marcel Breuer. Period drawing showing the houses' serial scheme and their bisected, pivoting floor plans. The third house shown in this plan was not built.

and a rear facade that flaunts framed outdoor rooms, exaggerated industrial-style outdoor staircases, and theatrically exposed cables.

In 1933 Sigfried Giedion recognized Breuer's constructivist predisposition and asked him to join Emil Roth in designing two houses for a property he owned in Doldertal, an exclusive section of Zurich. Giedion also invited ABC's newest affiliate, Alfred Roth, to join the team. Ten years younger than his cousin Emil (Alfred was born in 1903), he had studied with Karl Moser and graduated from the ETH in 1926. Regrettably there was much disagreement between Breuer and the Roths, but by 1936 the men had created two of the era's finest buildings.

Although the Doldertal houses are elegant villas for privileged residents, they reflect the ABC spirit nonetheless. Their facades maintain a constant dialogue between closed and open volumes, as each level emphasizes enclosed spaces and corresponding outdoor rooms punctuated by supporting columns. Furthermore, a highly visible industrial metal staircase, hardly suitable for villas, connects the third-floor terraces to the roofs. The plan of the Doldertal houses follows ABC precedent as well. From the street the houses give the impression of being single rectangular volumes, but actually both buildings have right-angled plans. What is unusual is the manner in which they are sited. The architects placed these buildings on active angles that imply partial rotation. The increasing sense of animation found in ABC designs of the 1930s is clearly apparent here.

Like Emil Roth's Deuchler House, the Doldertal houses simultaneously embrace and reject preciousness. In spite of their patrician image and locale, they are presented as virtually identical serial buildings. Clearly *ABC Beiträge zum Bauen*'s insistence on mass production and standardization was being heeded—in a hybrid post-1930 fashion.

The innovative quality of such buildings as the Deuchler and Doldertal houses, and their impressive number, lent a very optimistic tone to issue 5 of *Weiterbauen*. This issue led readers to believe that they were witnessing a surge of ABC-inspired building in Switzerland; even grander buildings might have been expected in forthcoming issues.

3

The Final Chapter, 1936–1939

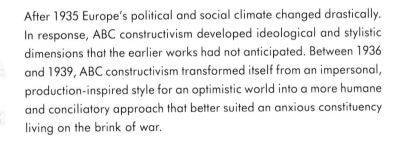

After 1935 Europe's political and social climate changed drastically. In response, ABC constructivism developed ideological and stylistic dimensions that the earlier works had not anticipated. Between 1936 and 1939, ABC constructivism transformed itself from an impersonal, production-inspired style for an optimistic world into a more humane and conciliatory approach that better suited an anxious constituency living on the brink of war.

During these years ABC buildings looked increasingly different from those of the previous decade. While it is true that architectural tastes had changed during the thirties, for most of the remaining ABC members the change in their own work was not purely an acquiescence to new tastes. As the ABC architects watched Adolf Hitler's political ascent and his insatiable territorial appetite, it became clear that the survival of Europe was in question. These architects consequently realized that ABC constructivism, in its original form, was no longer appropriate.

Whereas ABC constructivism of the early twenties had favored revolution and lionized the machine, after 1930 the remaining ABC architects—who were never particularly militant in the first place—reconsidered ABC's position. By the mid-thirties it was clear that they no longer wished to be associated with any militant stance. In fact, the ABC members were willing to go to great lengths to promote peaceful coexistence among parties who did not share common ideals. They were even prepared for some conciliation with the architects of the nationalistic right. *Weiterbauen*'s final issue proved this only too well.

The sixth and final issue appeared in December 1936. It had nothing in common with the optimistic spirit of issue 5. Until this time *Weiterbauen* had chosen, not very realistically, to disregard the encroaching menace of Heimatschutz. But by the winter of 1936 Heimatschutz had become so powerful and threatening that it had to be acknowledged by the publication.

Heimatschutz was a part of the nationalistic reaction that had overtaken Germany and was now sweeping Switzerland. It called for a return to traditional values and a vernacular architecture. Heimatschutz published its own periodicals and was successful among the Swiss populace. By 1936, the movement had gathered such momentum that it became a serious obstacle to the development of modernism.

Heimatschutz's leaders challenged the relevance of *Weiterbauen* and were prepared to launch a campaign against its architects. Were such strong radical fighters as Stam, Meyer, or Schmidt still leading ABC, it is probable that ABC would have stood up to Heimatschutz in print or by other means. Hans Schmidt did in fact recall incidents in which he and friends had organized to form militant brigades that verbally battled Heimatschutz personalities at public lectures.[4] Werner Moser, Haefeli, Steiger, and members of the Zurich core, however, had never been comfortable pursuing extreme positions and were hardly prepared to do so now. Conflict was not what they sought in these tense times. In 1936 they decided to make their peace with Heimatschutz, and they documented this in print.

Accordingly, *Weiterbauen* acknowledged Heimatschutz's leaders and attempted to find some measure of relevance in their position. In the opening article of issue 6, "Heimatschutz und neues Bauen," Ernst Burckhardt declared that not all of Heimatschutz was negative. There was in fact a "positive Heimatschutz" as well. Werner Moser explained that traditional vernacular types were valid if they were truly an honest expression of earlier indigenous prototypes. Moser urged some form of truce between the Swiss CIAM members and Heimatschutz. The magazine then chronicled how CIAM members, after accepting Moser's proposal, agreed to meet with representatives of the increasingly vociferous movement.[5]

Results of the meeting were presented in a format that recalled the black-rimmed obituary *ABC Beiträge zum Bauen* had employed in its evaluation of the *Schweizerische Bauzeitung* in its inaugural issue. Entitled "Resolution," the article detailed the group's bargain with the devil. It proclaimed that the Swiss CIAM circle and the Heimatschutz organization had agreed, in theory, to band together. CIAM representatives would seek active participation in Heimatschutz and in return the latter would take a more expansive interest in town planning and public housing.[6]

Several pages of photographs and text followed the "Resolution," reiterating that modernism was now merely an option. For each modernist design such as Neubühl, there were at least two traditional or neoclassical alternatives alongside it. There was little left to be said after issue 6; *Weiterbauen* ceased publication shortly thereafter.

The final issue of *Weiterbauen* permanently changed the course of ABC constructivism and hastened its demise. With issue 6, the ABC architects altered their focus and their style. The new spirit of compromise resulted in a degree of ecumenism and multivalency that was not previously possible. Although the ABC architects never resorted to a neoclassical or vernacular Heimatschutz imagery, they did modify the existing ABC vocabulary to suit their new position.

The original goal of ABC constructivism had been to create abstract edifices that boldly expressed technological innovation and represented an unrelenting position politically and stylistically. Now, however, with technology responsible for supplying the tools of aggression and hastening the probability of war, such inferences seemed incorrect. Furthermore, overwhelming, monolithic structures such as the Van Nelle factory and the Halle airport restaurant no longer seemed suitable. The scale of these buildings only heightened man's increasing feeling of helplessness in an already insecure world.

Seeking a relevant architectural response to the times, the ABC group sought to create a more humane architecture, an architecture that represented neither militancy, mechanization, singular viewpoints, nor overt monumentality. Consequently, Egender, Moser, Haefeli, and their colleagues resolved to produce less intimidating buildings that projected a more comfortable scale, a multivalent vocabulary, and a softened and changed constructivist imagery.

Freibad Allenmoos, a Zurich bathing club by Werner Moser and Max Ernst Haefeli of 1938–1939, illustrates this new attitude (plate 6). In many ways, the design of Bad Allenmoos is faithful to ABC tradition. The club is presented as a right-angled compound of pavilions each of which houses a different function. Exposed industrial stairwells, revealed structure, and dematerialized walls do appear throughout, but very significant changes are evident. Human comfort and the human relationship to nature overshadow all other agendas.

Architecture is no longer a raison d'être in its own right; it serves as a means for making man more comfortable in his surroundings.

The plan and design of the bathing club buildings (a restaurant, lockers, and game rooms) prove this point. The buildings are sited around an expansive green campus and a swimming pool. As one might expect of Werner Moser, lush landscaping features prominently. Previously, however, buildings had been the dominating presences within his schemes, while landscaping served as an accessory or backdrop. Here the roles are reversed, as the buildings are diminished in scale and mass while nature becomes increasingly powerful. To underscore nature's preeminence, Moser and Haefeli enclosed many spaces in walls of glass to allow the buildings to merge into the surrounding gardens (figure 6.7). Furthermore, much of the formal vocabulary used throughout is rounded and organic. Bad Allenmoos has numerous mushroom columns, curved roofs, circular stairwells, and round elements such as the kiosks that correspond to nature's shapes. Their curvilinear silhouettes allow the buildings to fuse with their environment rather than stand apart from it.

The organic forms also lend a relaxed, noninstitutional quality to the area, one that the scale and siting of the buildings echo. For example, the glass walls of many buildings do not resemble the monolithic ones seen at Halle, as they are divided into very small grid-shaped panels that are intimately scaled (figure 6.7). To enhance the relaxed feeling, the public buildings here are low-rise and not too large. A sense of flexibility also prevails as there is no single defining shape to the assorted pavilions; rectilinear ones coexist alongside curved ones. Nor is there a well-defined circulatory system linking the complex. Often only understated garden paths join buildings, and these do not necessarily meet, resulting in a casualness that is ground-breaking for ABC.

A calculated lightheartedness enters into the Bad Allenmoos scheme as well. This is particularly evident in the way Moser and Haefeli

6.7
Freibad Allenmoos, Zurich, 1938–1939, by Werner Moser and Max Ernst Haefeli. Interior view of the game room surrounded by grid-paneled windows. Current photo, © 1992 Walter Mair.

present one of the holiest points of the original style—the right-angled juncture. The restaurant terrace and the game room complex are, aside from the swimming pool, the focal structures of the Bad Allenmoos campus (see plate 6). Placed in right-angled formation, according to ABC tradition they should meet or intersect. But they do not. Instead, their anticipated point of juncture unexpectedly features a curved staircase that lightly floats between them in a playful, teasing manner. The sanctity of the ABC canon is challenged as Bad Allenmoos dismantles many of its tenets in a fashion unthinkable years earlier.

The Johanniskirche by Egender and Burckhardt, a Protestant church in Basel that was completed in 1936, illustrates the dissolution of ABC constructivism in another fashion. Anything but a single cohesive edifice, this church is an amalgam of distinct parts that are not necessarily related to one another physically or visually. As a result, the strength of the building lies not in its larger whole, as was the case in buildings such as the Halle airport restaurant, but in its parts and details. The trend toward diffraction and multivalent imagery that had begun after 1930 is fully apparent here.

The Johanniskirche is a complex consisting of a church building, rectory, and seemingly freestanding bell tower. All three appear to be stylistically unrelated. The rectory is spartan, built of plain dark brick and structurally inarticulate. The church is its exact opposite, a study in decoration, surprising contrasts, and structure. Exposed vertical beams support a canopy that leads into the church. Utilitarian, they contrast with the facade, which is covered in a decorative arrangement of grid patterns (figure 6.8). The same type of juxtaposition occurs in the interior, where industrial metal beams are exposed against rich walls of marble (figure 6.9).

The church and the rectory are placed next to each other at right angles, but once again do not actually connect. This deliberate sense of disconnection is echoed by the design and placement of the bell tower, here treated as a freestanding structure that is stylistically and almost physically independent (figure 6.10).

The bell tower is the dominant constructivist element within the Johanniskirche. It is one of the finest and purest constructivist statements found anywhere within the spectrum of the ABC movement. Conceptually it dates back to the reductivist constructivism of Lamstov and Simbirchev, as it consists solely of three vividly exposed parts: bold open frame, a striking industrial spiral staircase, and a utilitarian bell. So masterful is their arrangement that the bell tower deserves to be seen as a dynamic piece of sculpture in its own right. Clearly Egender was eminently capable of creating excellent constructivist designs when he chose to do so. The fact that only one part of this complex was decidedly constructivist was not due to a lack of ability on the architect's part. Reduction of constructivist content was Egender's way of announcing that the constructivist era had reached its final stage and was being phased out.

6.8
St. Johannes, Basel, 1936,
by Karl Egender and E. F.
Burckhardt. Entry to the
church building with church
facade in rear. Current photo,
© 1992 Walter Mair.

6.9
St. Johannes, Basel, 1936,
by Karl Egender and E. F.
Burckhardt. Interior view
of exposed columns against
marble walls. Current photo,
© 1992 Walter Mair.

6.10
St. Johannes, Basel, 1936,
by Karl Egender and E. F.
Burckhardt. The bell tower.
Current photo, 1992 Walter
Mair.

Egender's Oerlikon Stadium, designed and built in Zurich between 1936 and 1938 in collaboration with the engineer R. Naef, is even stronger in its reduction of constructivist content. A covered hexagonal stadium of reinforced concrete for 11,000 persons, it encloses the boldest ABC interior since the Halle airport restaurant. Within the main space, exposed 280-foot trusses of steel are suspended from a dropped ceiling and unquestionably become the distinguishing features of the 100,000-square-foot space. The interior's constructivist impact is, however, carried over to only one of the exterior's six facades.

Oerlikon is an exceptionally powerful statement without a focal image. Each of the six sides shares such common features as exposed pipes, upper-story windows, a degree of exposed structure, and brick infill panels. However, each facade differs from the next. In Gaudiesque fashion, the facades seem in a constant state of metamorphosis as they encircle the stadium. They progress from the planar and ethereal, in which there are large panels of glass, flat walls, and attenuated structural members (figure 6.11), to a massive, three-dimensional constructivist section where windows become smaller, ledges cantilever, walls belly, and structural supports grow increasingly muscular as they rise (figure 6.12). The transitions between these facades are remarkably fluid. Windows do not suddenly change from the large to the small; rather they graduate in size before and after they turn corners. As a result, there is a graceful flow from one facade into the next and a sense of organic cohesion in what might otherwise have been a visually confusing exterior.

The variety of the facades prevents this huge edifice from projecting a monolithic, overbearing image—or a complete constructivist one, as true constructivist presentation is limited to one facade. Only on this facade do the exterior supports reach maximal size and strength in a dramatically overt manner. And yet, on the basis of the interior and this facade the Oerlikon Stadium must be considered an ABC landmark. Few buildings built at any time during ABC's history expose structural elements as boldly or as adroitly as they do.

6.11
Oerlikon Stadium, Zurich,
1933, by Karl Egender and R.
Naef. A facade. Current photo,
1992 Walter Mair.

6.12
Oerlikon Stadium, Zurich, 1938, by Karl Egender and R. Naef. The most constructivist of the stadium's six facades. Current photo, 1992 Walter Mair.

Regrettably, it was the increasing dissolution of ABC constructivism that finally led to its demise. The Johanniskirche, Bad Allenmoos, and the Oerlikon Stadium were public edifices that intimated that the original ABC style was no longer viable and needed to be replaced by a less doctrinaire approach. Accordingly, the ABC architects made increasingly drastic changes. In Bad Allenmoos the style's very nature was altered. In Egender's buildings it was gradually phased out: at the Johanniskirche constructivism represented one out of three exterior parts, and at the later Oerlikon Stadium only one out of six. In any percentage beyond that, the constructivist content could no longer be seen as a significant identifying element.

The Oerlikon Stadium proved to be the swan song of ABC constructivism. After Oerlikon, ABC's remaining Swiss architects, while continuing to employ structural systems that were common to the ABC approach, no longer made the effort to perpetuate the style in its own right. The designs Egender unveiled immediately after Oerlikon prove this only too well, particularly those he designed for the national exhibition of 1939, the Landesausstellung in Zurich. Clearly missing here was an attempt to make a constructivist statement. Though he used space-age imagery and exposed technological parts in the exhibition's revolving restaurant, the effect was lighthearted and worthy of an amusement park. The same sensation was projected by his Modepavillon, which assumed the form of three huge teepees. Decoration, visual variety, and amusing forms so overwhelmed Egender's otherwise well-articulated pavilions that any sense of ideological commitment, if intended, was lost.

From 1939 onward, what remained of ABC constructivism merged with mainstream Swiss modernism. After the Second World War, the ABC movement became a memory as Alfred Roth, Werner Moser, Max Ernst Haefeli, and Rudolf Steiger became commercially successful modernists in their homeland. They also remained active within CIAM, whose impact lasted for several generations. Throughout the span of their lives, these men remained highly respected members of Switzerland's architectural community.[7]

Unfortunately, the same was not true for Stam, Wittwer, Meyer, and Schmidt, ABC's founding luminaries. After returning from Russia, these architects were marked as Communists and could not properly reestablish themselves in Western Europe. They eventually detached themselves from relevant architectural circles. By the 1940s they were rarely heard from. Wittwer and Stam grew reclusive, Schmidt devoted his time to teaching in East Germany, and Meyer remained a town planner in Mexico.

It is due in large part to their exile or self-exile that ABC's legacy was never brought to proper public attention. Meyer, Stam, Wittwer, and Schmidt were the only ABC members in a position fully to outline the ideological and practical goals as well as the works of the ABC movement. Other ABC members could not accurately provide this information. Werner Moser had been out of the country during ABC's formative years and Egender, Haefeli, and Steiger first became involved after 1927. Alfred Roth did not affiliate himself with the group until the thirties. That left Emil Roth; but while he had been a noteworthy figure in 1924, he later lacked the prominence to qualify as a spokesman. After the mid-thirties his career waned, and his diminished standing in Switzerland's architectural circles left him in relative obscurity for generations.[8]

As there was no one prominent enough or sufficiently informed to promote ABC constructivism after World War II, a great deal about the movement was lost to international architecture. The ideology and designs that defined ABC constructivism were increasingly forgotten. It is the intention of this book to rectify this situation, presenting the ABC legacy in its entirety so that ABC may finally assume its place in the history of modernism.

Notes

One

1

For an overview of Russian constructivist architecture as well as the propaganda potential inherent in Russia's graphics, art forms, and architectural visions between 1918 and 1924, see Anatole Kopp, *Town and Revolution: Soviet Architecture and City Planning, 1917–1935*, trans. Thomas Burton (New York: George Braziller, 1970), chapters 1–4.

2

The activities of the International Faction of Constructivists as well as Lissitzky's address to the International Congress of Progressive Artists are documented in Stephen Bann, *The Tradition of Constructivism* (London: Thames and Hudson, 1974), pp. 58–69.

3

The "Proun" lecture Lissitzky delivered was written between 1920 and 1921. It was again given at the Moscow Institute for Artistic Culture on October 23, 1924, when he briefly returned to the Soviet Union. The lecture is reprinted in its entirety in Galerie Gmurzynska, *El Lissitzky* (Cologne, 1976), pp. 60–72.

4

Mart Stam, "Op zoek naar een abc van het bouwen" (In Search of the ABC of Building), in *Het Bouwbedrijf*, Amsterdam, no. 3 (1926), pp. 378 and 521. English translation appears in Gerrit Oorthuys, *Mart Stam: A Documentation of His Work 1920–1965* (London: RIBA Publications, 1970), p. 6.

5

Mart Stam, "Holland und die Baukunst unserer Zeit" (Holland and the Architecture of Our Time), *Schweizerische Bauzeitung*, 82, no. 15 (October 1923), pp. 1–4. This translation and all subsequent translations from the German are by the author.

6

Mart Stam, "Holland und die Baukunst unsere Zeit" (II), *Schweizerische Bauzeitung*, 82, no. 18 (November 1923), p. 1.

7

Ibid., pp. 1, 3.

8

Mart Stam, "El Lissitzky's Conception of Architecture" (1966), in Sophie Lissitzky-Küppers, *El Lissitzky: Life, Letters, Text* (Greenwich: New York Graphic Society, 1968), pp. 388–390.

Two

1

Hans Schmidt, "The Swiss Modern Movement 1920–1930," *Architectural Association Quarterly*, 4, no. 2 (April-June 1972), pp. 32–41.

2

Karl Moser as a member of the Swiss Werkbund was entitled to the publication of his work in *Das Werk*, the organization's official magazine. See Karl Moser, "Neue holländische Architektur, Bauten von W. M. Dudok—Hilversum" (The New Dutch Architecture, the Buildings of W. M. Dudok—Hilversum), *Das Werk*, 9, no. 11 (1922), pp. 205–214.

3

This information is based on a December 23, 1976, letter on the origins of ABC from Alfred Roth to the author. An interview of Emil Roth by the author during July 1978 corroborated these facts.

4

Hans Schmidt, "Genf: Wettbewerbsentwurf für das internationale Arbeitsamt" (Geneva: Competition Entry for the International Workers' Bureau), *ABC Beiträge zum Bauen* (Basel), series 2, no. 3 (1926), p. 5.

5

The four installments of Mart Stam's "Holland und die Baukunst unserer Zeit" appeared respectively in the *Schweizerische Bauzeitung* in vol. 82, no. 15 (October 13, 1923); vol. 82, no. 18 (November 3, 1923); vol. 82, no. 19 (November 10, 1923); and vol. 82, no. 21 (November 24, 1923).

6

E. Wipf, "Holland und die Baukunst unserer Zeit," *Schweizerische Bauzeitung*, 82, no. 24 (December 15, 1923), pp. 317–318.

7

Armin Meili, "Wir und die Architektur des Auslands" (Foreign Architecture and Us), *Schweizerische Bauzeitung*, 83, no. 1 (January 5, 1924), pp. 5–7.

8

Armin Meili, "Wir und die Architektur des Auslands," *Schweizerische Bauzeitung*, 83, no. 2 (January 12, 1924), pp. 20–22.

9

"Amerika," *ABC*, series 1, no. 1 (1924), p. 1.

10

Werner Moser, "Frank Lloyd Wright und amerikanische Architektur," *Das Werk*, 5 (1925), pp. 129–142.

Three

1

El Lissitzky, "Element und Erfindung" (Element and Invention), *ABC*, series 1, no. 1 (1924), p. 3.

2

El Lissitzky and Mart Stam, "Die Reklame" (Advertisement), *ABC*, series 1, no. 2 (1924), p. 3; El Lissitzky, shown without a caption, "The Constructor," series 1, no. 3/4 (1925), p. 8; El Lissitzky, "Rednertribune, 1926" (Speaker's Tribune), series 2, no. 1 (1926), p. 8; El Lissitzky, "Prounenraum" (Proun Room), series 2, no. 2 (1926), p. 3.

3

ABC, series 1, no. 2 (1924), p. 4.

4

El Lissitzky, quote from *Merz*, in *ABC*, series 1, no. 3/4 (1925), p. 12. El Lissitzky, "Rad, Propeller und das Folgende," originally in *G*, 1, no. 2 (September 1923), p. 2; in *ABC*, series 2, no. 1 (1926), p. 3. Hans Richter's film stills first appeared in *G*, 1, no. 1 (July 1923), p. 3; they were later shown in *ABC*, series 2, no. 1 (1926), p. 4.

5

Mart Stam and El Lissitzky, "Architektur Russlands" (Russian Architecture), *ABC*, series 1, no. 3/4 (1925), pp. 1–2.

6

Mart Stam and Hans Schmidt, "Das Volumen" (The Volume), *ABC*, series 1, no. 5 (1925), p. 4.

7

"Turm zur Verarbeitung von Lauge" (Tower for the Production of Lye), *ABC*, series 1, no. 3/4 (1925), p. 2. "Restaurant an einem Felsen über Meer" (Restaurant on a Cliff over a Lake), ibid., p. 3. The architects' names are not given for either project. They are credited only as coming from Atelier Ladovsky at the Vkhutemas in Moscow.

8

"Modell Flugplatzgestaltung—Atelier Ladowski" (Airport Model—Atelier Ladovsky), *ABC*, series 1, no. 6 (1925), p. 1. L. Popova and A. Vesnin, "Fliegende Propaganda" (Flying Propaganda), *ABC*, series 2, no. 1 (1926), p. 3.

9

School for Boys, St. Wendel's, Germany, 1924, project by Mart Stam in *Het Bouwbedrijf*, 3 (1928), pp. 523–524. School in Thun, Switzerland, 1925, project by Mart Stam in *Het Bouwbedrijf*, 5 (1928), p. 185.

10

Based on an interview with Emil Roth in Zurich during July 1978. El Lissitzky corroborates this information in Lissitzky-Küppers, *El Lissitzky*, pp. 56–58.

11

According to an interview with Moser's widow during July 1978, her husband sent this information and the accompanying photographs and drawings to Schmidt and Stam while he was in the United States. See "Stahlgerippe eines Wolkenkratzers in Baltimore" (Steel Skeleton of a Skyscraper in Baltimore), in *ABC*, series 1, no. 2 (1924), p. 3; "Mechanische Autogaragen" (Mechanized Automobile Garage), *ABC*, series 2, no. 3 (1926), p. 4.

12

Claude Schnaidt, *Hannes Meyer: Buildings, Projects and Writings* (Teufen: Verlag Arthur Niggli, 1965), p. 25.

13

Ibid.

Four

1

"Kunst," *ABC*, series 2, no. 4 (1927/28), p. 12.

2

Schmidt, "The Swiss Modern Movement," p. 37.

3

Mart Stam, "Wohnhäuser Stuttgart 1927" (Homes, Stuttgart, 1927), *ABC*, series 2, no. 4 (1927–1928), p. 6.

4

Hans Schmidt, "Typengrundrisse" (Standardized Plans) and "Wohnkolonie" (Residence Colony), *ABC*, series 2, no. 4 (1927–1928), p. 7.

5

Emil Roth, "Gelände und Bebauung am Zürichsee" (Land and Development by the Zürichsee), *ABC*, series 1, no. 5 (1925), pp. 1–2.

6

Hans Schmidt, "Technische und wirtschaftliche Resultate eines Wohnhausbaues" (The Technical and Economic Results of a Residential Building Method), *ABC*, series 2, no. 4 (1927–1928), p. 9.

7

Mart Stam, "Modernes Bauen 3" (Modern Building 3), *ABC*, series 1, no. 3/4 (1925), pp. 3–5.

8

Hans Schmidt, "Le Corbusier als Architekt und Schriftsteller," 1927, in Bruno Flierl, *Hans Schmidt, Beiträge zur Architektur 1924–1964* (Berlin: Verlag für Bauwesen, 1965), pp. 27–28.

Five

1

In a letter dated June 10, 1964, Mart Stam admitted to designing the Kees van der Leeuw House and the house in Ommen and to being the designer in charge of the Van Nelle factory, despite the fact that the firm of Brinkman and Van der Vlugt took the credit for the building. This letter is reprinted in Gerrit Oorthuys, *Mart Stam: A Documentation of His Work 1920–1965* (London: RIBA Publications, 1970), p. 40.

2

Schnaidt, *Hannes Meyer: Buildings, Projects and Writings*, p. 41.

3

From an interview between Hannes Meyer and Pravda correspondent A. Gatman on October 10, 1930. See Kopp, *Town and Revolution*, p. 258.

4

Hans Schmidt, "Wer für wen" (Who for Whom), 1931, in Flierl, *Hans Schmidt, Beiträge zur Architektur*, p. 82.

5

Mart Stam, "Holland und die Baukunst unserer Zeit IV," *Schweizerische Bauzeitung*, 82 (November 1923), p. 271.

6

Hans Schmidt, "Das Chaos im Stadtbau" (The Chaos in City Planning), *ABC*, series 1, no. 1 (1924), pp. 2–4.

7

Mart Stam, "Trautenau," *ABC*, series 2, no. 1 (1926), p. 7.

8

Klaus Jürgen Winkler, *Der Architekt Hannes Meyer, Anschauungen und Werk* (Berlin: VEB Verlag, 1989), pp. 131–181, provides a thorough review of Meyer's life and work in the Soviet Union.

9

In his monograph on Mart Stam, Gerrit Oorthuys provides an overview of Stam's activities in the USSR, particularly of his work in Magnitogorsk and Makeyevka. See Oorthuys, *Mart Stam: A Documentation of His Work*, pp. 24–29.

10

Hans Schmidt, "Was ist richtig?" (What Is Right?), 1933, in Flierl, *Hans Schmidt, Beiträge zur Architektur*, pp. 90–91.

11

Hans Schmidt, "Die sowjetische Architektur und das Problem des Monumentalen" (Soviet Architecture and the Problem of Monumentality), 1937, in Flierl, *Hans Schmidt*, pp. 115–120.

12

Paul Artaria, *Vom Bauen und Wohnen* (Basel: Wepf Verlag, 1948). Paul Artaria died in 1959.

Six

1

For a review of the ABC group's assertiveness at the first CIAM conference at La Sarraz, see Sigfried Giedion, "International Vereinigung des neues Bauen" (The International Congress for Modern Architecture), *Schweizerische Bauzeitung*, 92 (1928), pp. 47–48, and Martin Steinmann, *CIAM-Dokumente 1928–1939* (Basel: Birkhauser Verlag, 1979), pp. 15, 22–25.

2

Alfred Roth, "Das Dachgeschoss und seine Ausnutzung" (The Roof Frame and Its Uses), *Weiterbauen* (Zurich), 1 (September 1934), pp. 5–7.

3

Marcel Breuer's constructivist phase and his design for the Doldertal houses are discussed in Magdalena Droste and Manfred Ludewig, *Marcel Breuer Design* (Cologne: Benedikt Taschen Verlag, 1992), pp. 25–28.

4

Hans Schmidt, "The Swiss Modern Movement," p. 39.

5

Ernst Burckhardt, "Heimatschutz und neues Bauen" (Heimatschutz and the New Architecture), *Weiterbauen*, 6 (December 1936), pp. 1–3.

6

"Resolution," ibid., p. 4.

7

Max Ernst Haefeli, Werner Moser, and Rudolf Steiger were active partners throughout the 1930s. Their partnership lasted and gained in prestige through the 1960s. During those years the partners designed numerous commercial buildings, including Bally-Haus, in Zurich, which was completed in 1968. Haefeli, Moser, and Steiger were revered by the ETH and the Swiss architectural establishment until their deaths. Moser died in 1970, Haefeli in 1976, and Steiger in 1982.

Karl Egender enjoyed success as well after 1940, though not quite on the scale of Haefeli, Moser, and Steiger. He continued to design and build and in 1940 became a professor at the ETH. In 1950 he assumed the presidency of the GSMBA, a prestigious Swiss architectural organization. He died in 1969.

Alfred Roth lives in Zurich. Since the 1940s he has come to be regarded as one of the founding fathers of Swiss modernism. He has taught at the ETH, written articles and books on modern architecture, and designed numerous schools and buildings in Europe. Roth has also designed schools and entire communities throughout the Middle East.

8

After 1940 Emil Roth's career as a practicing architect declined, partly due to ill health. In addition to designing some small buildings, he supported himself and his family by teaching at the Gewerbeschule (crafts school) in Zurich between 1940 and 1959. He died in 1980.

Bibliography

Architects

The following listing is of biographies, autobiographies, and articles that address biographical issues and present either an entire or a partial overview of the oeuvre of individual ABC architects.

Artaria, Paul. **Vom Bauen und Wohnen.** Basel: Wepf Verlag, 1948.

Birnholz, Alan. "El Lissitzky." Dissertation, Yale University, 1973.

Flierl, Bruno. **Hans Schmidt, Beiträge zur Architektur 1924–1964.** Berlin: Verlag für Bauwesen, 1965.

Galerie Gmurzynska. **El Lissitzky.** Cologne, 1976.

"Haefeli, Moser, Steiger." **Architese,** 10, no. 2 (March-April 1980). The entire issue.

Hannes Meyer: Architekt, Urbanist, Lehrer, 1889–1954. Berlin: Ernst und Sohn, 1989. Anthology.

Hays, K. Michael. **Modernism and the Posthumanist Subject: The Architecture of Hannes Meyer and Ludwig Hilberseimer.** Cambridge: MIT Press, 1992.

Kieren, Martin. **Hannes Meyer, Architekt.** Heiden: Verlag Arthur Niggli, 1990.

Krucker, Bruno, and Markus Wassmer. **Zwischen den Zeilen: Die Vision und ihre Transformation Karl Egenders, vom Haus Büchner 1925 zur Landi 1939.** Qualifying paper. Zurich: GTA/The Federal Institute of Technology, 1985.

Lissitzky, El. **Proun und Wolkenbügel: Schriften, Briefe, Dokumente.** Dresden: VEB Verlag, 1977.

Lissitzky-Küppers, Sophie. **El Lissitzky: Life, Letters, Text.** Greenwich: New York Graphic Society, 1968.

Oorthuys, Gerrit. **Mart Stam: A Documentation of His Work 1920–1965.** London: RIBA Publications, 1970.

Roth, Alfred. **The New Architecture 1930–1940.** Zurich: Verlag Artemis, 1975.

Rummele, Simone. **Mart Stam.** Zurich: Artemis und Winkler, 1991.

Schmidt, Hans. "The Swiss Modern Movement 1920–1930." **Architectural Association Quarterly,** 4, no. 2 (April–June 1972), pp. 32–41.

Schnaidt, Claude. **Hannes Meyer: Buildings, Projects and Writings.** Teufen: Verlag Arthur Niggli, 1965.

Senn, Otto. "Hans Schmidt 1892–1972." **Werk,** 59, no. 10 (October 1972), pp. 548–562.

Winkler, Klaus Jürgen. **Der Architekt Hannes Meyer, Anschauungen und Werk.** Berlin: VEB Verlag, 1989.

Wittwer, Hans-Jacob. **Hans Wittwer (1894–1952).** Zurich: GTA Verlag, 1985.

Texts on ABC, the ABC Period, and ABC Architects

ABC Beiträge zum Bauen. Series 1, no. 1 (1924), Zurich. Series 1, nos. 2–6 (1924–1925), Basel. Series 2, nos. 1–4 (1926–1928), Basel.

ABC Beiträge zum Bauen. Reprint. Eindhoven: Technische Hogeschool Eindhoven,1969.

Bann, Stephen. **The Tradition of Constructivism.** London: Thames and Hudson, 1974.

Bayer, Herbert, Ise Gropius, and Walter Gropius. **Bauhaus 1919–1928.** New York: Museum of Modern Art, 1938.

Burckhardt, Julius, ed. **The Werkbund: History and Ideology 1907–1933.** New York : Barrons, 1980.

Campbell, Joan. **The German Werkbund: The Politics of Reform in the Applied Arts.** Princeton: Princeton University Press, 1978.

Campi, Mario. **Weiterbauen weiter.** Zurich: ETH, 1977.

Diserens, Anne-Lise. **Zuerich.** Zurich: ETH, 1988.

Droste, Magdalena. **Bauhaus.** Berlin: Bauhaus Archiv, 1990.

Droste, Magdalena, Manfred Ludewig, and the Bauhaus-Archiv. **Marcel Breuer Design.** Cologne: Benedikt Taschen Verlag, 1992.

Frampton, Kenneth. "The New Objectivity: Germany, Holland and Switzerland 1923–1933." In **Modern Architecture, a Critical History.** New York: Oxford University Press, 1980.

G—Zeitschrift für Elementare Gestaltung. Berlin, Nos 1–6, 1923–1926.

Graf, Urs, ed. **Neues Bauen in der Schweiz.** Blauen: Schweizer Baudokumentation, 1985.

Grinberg, Donald. **Housing in the Netherlands 1900–1940.** Delft: Delft University Press, 1982.

Gropius, Walter. **Idee und Aufbau des staatliches Bauhauses Weimar.** Munich: Bauhausverlag, 1923.

Gubler, Jacques. **ABC, Achitettura e Avanguardia 1924–1928.** Milan: Electa, 1983.

Gubler, Jacques. **Nationalisme et internationalisme dans l'architecture moderne de la Suisse.** Lausanne: Editions L'Age d'Homme, 1975.

Hitchcock, Henry-Russell, and Philip Johnson. **The International Style.** New York: Norton and Company, 1966.

Joedicke, Jürgen, and Christian Plath. **Die Weissenhofsiedlung Stuttgart.** Stuttgart: Karl Kramer Verlag, 1977.

Jones, Cranston. **Marcel Breuer: Buildings and Projects 1921–1962.** New York: Frederick Praeger, 1962.

Juda, Annely. **The First Russian Show.** London: Annely Juda Fine Art, 1983.

Kidder-Smith, G. E. **Switzerland Builds.** New York: Albert Bonnier, 1950.

Kirsch, Karin. **Die Weissenhofsiedlung.** Stuttgart: Deutsche Verlags-Anstalt, 1987.

Lane, Barbara Miller. **Architecture and Politics in Germany 1918–1945.** Cambridge: Harvard University Press, 1985.

Neue Nationalgalerie Berlin. **Tendenzen der zwanziger Jahre.** Berlin: Dietrich Reimer Verlag, 1977.

Noseda, Irma, and Martin Steinmann. **Zeitzeichen.** Zurich: Verlag der Akademischen Technischen Vereine Zurich, 1988

Roth, Alfred. **The New Architecture 1930–1940.** Zurich: Artemis Verlag, 1975.

Sharon, Arieh. **Kibbutz and Bauhaus.** Stuttgart: Karl Kramer Verlag, 1976.

Staber, Margit. **Um 1930 in Zürich.** Zurich: Kunstgewerbe Museum Zürich, 1977.

Steinmann, Martin. **CIAM, Dokumente 1928–1939.** Basel: Birkhauser Verlag, 1978.

Veshch, Gegenstand, Objet. Issues 1–3 (1922), Berlin: Skythen Verlag.

Weiterbauen. Issues 1–6 (1934–1936), Zurich: Deren Verlag.

Willet, John. **Art and Politics in the Weimar Period.** New York: Pantheon, 1978.

Wingler, Hans. **Bauhaus.** Cambridge: MIT Press, 1969.

Texts on Russian Constructivism and Asnova

Barron, Stephanie, and Maurice Tuchman. **The Avante-Garde in Russia 1910–1930: New Perspectives.** Cambridge: MIT Press, 1980.

Chan-Magomedow, S. O. **Pionere der sowjetischen Architektur.** Vienna: Locker Verlag, 1983.

Cohen, J. L., M. Michelis, and M. Tafuri. **URSS 1917–1978 : la ville, l'architecture.** Paris: L'Equerre, 1979

Frampton, Kenneth. "Notes on Soviet Urbanism 1917–1932." **Architects Yearbook 12.** London, 1968.

Kopp, Anatole. **Constructivist Architecture in the USSR.** London: Academy Editions, 1985

Kopp, Anatole. **Town and Revolution: Soviet Architecture and City Planning, 1917–1935.** Trans. Thomas Burton. New York: George Braziller, 1970

Lodder, Christina. **Russian Constructivism.** New Haven: Yale University Press, 1983.

Shvidkovsky, O. A. **Building in the USSR.** New York: Praeger, 1971.

Index